PRAISE FOR *LODESTAR*

"Throughout my career, I have understood the value of practical wisdom and scientific analysis. The balance struck between timeless principles and exclusive interviews, makes *Lodestar* a uniquely powerful guide to real-world applications for those in pursuit of personal and professional growth."

—**JAMIE DIMON, Chairman and CEO of JPMorgan Chase & Co.**

"*Lodestar* is like having two friendly guides walk you through the distilled wisdom of the past several decades on how you can live your best life, both personally and professionally. You will gain valuable insight guaranteed. *Lodestar* feels familiar because so many of its lessons ring so true."

—**ANDREW YANG, Founder of Forward Party, Presidential Candidate in 2020**

"*Lodestar* is the rare book providing life guidance over career, character, company, and community domains, transporting the reader magically across such perspectives without ever seeming preachy or judgmental. The book is not a script of truisms but a compass that helps you find a path unique to your own goals. It introduces new ideas in a manner that shows insight and appreciation of different strategic contexts and personal priorities. As a result, Jim McCann's own rare empathetic qualities show us how to understand others before we condemn them or worship them. The lessons are clear, but like the varied viewers of any great work of art, they will have different meanings for each reader."

—**PROFESSOR JEFFREY SONNENFELD, Lester Crown Professor at Yale School of Management**

"The authors have gone beyond the ordinary, weaving together the best ideas of the past and presenting them alongside exclusive interviews with those who have turned theory into triumph. *Lodestar* is not just a book; it is a shortcut to the elusive path of career and individual growth."

—MARK VICTOR HANSEN, Founder and Cocreator of the *Chicken Soup for the Soul* Book Series

"For as long as I can remember, the presence of Jim McCann in the 1970s on television, his invitational warmth, and his sincerity always transmitted beyond mere business. We 'knew' him! He was a welcoming neighbor and compassionate friend. Amid the nearly five decades, a personal brethrenship has begun between us, and I can affirm the consistency of his rich heart, dedication, and contribution to the wellness of others, which match those from whom I come. He is a consummate discoverer of human nature and ways the 'plenty' can benefit. His journeys and new wisdoms through *Lodestar* will serve as an essential glossary for life's winning pathways, I am certain. Count me in for the revelations!"

—AMBASSADOR SHABAZZ, Diplomat, Lecturer, Consultant, Professor, and eldest daughter of Malcolm X

"As someone who has navigated the complexities of both Wall Street and Washington, I appreciate the clear road map *Lodestar* offers for achieving success. Jim McCann and George S. Everly, Jr. have crafted a guide that not only draws upon historical wisdom but also incorporates modern insights, including some from my own journey. This book is an invaluable asset for anyone looking to enrich themselves."

—ANTHONY SCARAMUCCI, Founder and Managing Partner, SkyBridge; Founder and Chairman, SALT

JIM McCANN

GEORGE S. EVERLY Jr., PhD, FAPA

LODESTAR

TAPPING INTO THE 10 TIMELESS
PILLARS OF SUCCESS

Lodestar: Tapping into the 10 Timeless Pillars of Success

Copyright © 2024 by Jim McCann and George S. Everly Jr., PhD, FAPA

Published by Worth Books, an imprint of Forefront Books, Nashville, Tennessee.
Distributed by Simon & Schuster.

Library of Congress Control Number: 2024904541

Print ISBN: 978-1-63763-273-4
E-book ISBN: 978-1-63763-274-1

Cover Design by Elisha Zepeda, Faceout Studios
Interior Design by Bill Kersey, KerseyGraphics

Printed in the United States of America

DEDICATIONS

Jim McCann

Having the opportunity to work on this book with my friend George Everly has been a real treat. It's a continuation of my lifelong learning process and finding a way to be in the company of smart, thoughtful, and good people, and George is certainly all of that.

We connected at the beginning of COVID and developed a relationship that became a friendship before we ever met in person. Now that we've met in person, it's ruined! ☺

I was flattered and thrilled when George asked me to work on this project with him. It has been an accelerated path of learning and certainly a good deal of work. But George did the heavy lifting, and I so enjoyed our working sessions because they were, for me, advanced learning sessions.

The coordinator of this project, Lisa Sabat, was new to our team when this idea was born. Well, she certainly doesn't feel new to the team now. She guided us with an understated doggedness and determination. She made the process fun, and she genuinely earned the nickname that one of her team members gave her, which is the Velvet Steamroller. She kept us on plan, focused, and on schedule with a fierce determination to get the best out of us.

As I think back to all the wonderful people I've had the opportunity to get to know, work with, and learn from over the years, the team that I'm surrounded by today is remarkable. Patty Altadonna, my work partner for thirty-one years; Lisa Modica, who has been with us a dozen years; and now Lisa Sabat, who succeeded Meredith Weinberg, coming up on two years. They are wonderful, smart, hardworking people who are fun to be around. They make what we do seem easy, and they all have their subtle ways of keeping me on track. I'm so lucky to work with this talented group of people.

And none of the learning adventures I've been on would be possible without an understanding, thoughtful, tolerant wife and family. Marylou, my kids, and now my grandkids are my inspiration, my support, and the audience I want most to make proud.

George S. Everly Jr., PhD, FAPA
To Andi Everly and Peter Sullivan, Olivia Bernhardt, Bentley Bernhardt, George S. Everly IV, and Henry Paul Everly. Read this book! From the abyss of COVID-19 emerged a friendship with a truly remarkable man—Jim McCann. entrepreneur and philanthropist, Jim's wisdom is surpassed only by his compassion. Thank you, Jim.

CONTENTS

INTRODUCTION

lodestar [löd–stär]
n., one that leads, inspires, guides

WE'RE ALL ON A QUEST TO BE BETTER. IT'S AN ENDLESS JOURNEY, on which status and station do not matter. Most of us—regardless of our circumstances—believe we can overcome hardship and even turn our far-flung dreams into reality. We believe we can thrive and flourish, if only we find the right resources, insights, or path.

Our buying habits are proof. "Self-help" is one of the most popular literary genres of all time. Each year, readers buy eighteen million copies of self-help titles, resulting in an industry worth more than $10 billion.[1]

But the search for better—the desire to thrive and flourish—isn't a new phenomenon. Not at all.

People have been attempting to do better for as long as humans have been around. The most popular book of all time, the Bible, has a self-improvement bent to it, as do most other religious and spiritual texts. You'll find self-help-esque advice embedded in ancient philosophical teachings, from Buddhism to Stoicism. You'll even find it in fairy tales.

About one hundred years before the Brothers Grimm penned stories such as "Rapunzel," "Little Red Riding Hood," and "The Frog Prince," a man named Charles Perrault published a collection of European folklore stories. His book, *Stories or Tales from Past Times*, actually established the fairy-tale genre. But he didn't do it with the aim of launching the careers of a thousand Disney princess impersonators or selling merchandise on a global scale. Perrault's goal was to educate and foster self-improvement and self-determination, and that became the role of fairy tales: to teach us how to do better for ourselves. He was on to something—to truly teach life lessons, they have to be couched in entertaining stories or relatable anecdotes.

Flash-forward a century or so to December of 1812. The Brothers Grimm made their literary debut with a collection of eighty-six fairy tales called *Children's and Household Tales*. The stories were ostensibly intended to foster self-improvement by teaching valuable lessons about life and personal growth; many of them have since become iconic. But one of the most powerful is also among the least known: "The Story of the Youth Who Went Forth to Learn What Fear Was." It tells the tale of a boy who repeatedly finds himself in categorically frightening situations yet never once experiences fear.

Why is it so important?

It urges us to challenge our preconceived notion that fear, anxiety, and panic are necessary and inescapable consequences of adversity or threatening situations. By questioning our self-debilitating assumptions about life, we ultimately learn a lesson that philosophers and psychologists attempt to impart today: that people are disturbed not by things or experiences but by their interpretation of them. Or, as John Milton once noted, the mind is its own place and "can make a Heaven of a Hell or a Hell of a Heaven."[2] When we know that to be true, we are ultimately freed from the incapacitating burden of fear itself. All that's left is opportunity.

This, of course, is a key tenet of the modern self-improvement era, which came into being in 1859, when Samuel Smiles wrote a book that would change everything. It was titled *Self-Help*.

In 1912, Dale Carnegie began teaching classes on business education in New York City. His teachings led to the 1936 publication of the first major international bestselling self-help book, *How to Win Friends and Influence People*. A year later, Napoleon Hill released *Think and Grow Rich*. The self-help literary genre was off and running. Its popularity only continues to grow. But, as you might guess, not all of it has been that helpful.

Like any industry that promises big returns for both purveyors and customers, self-help has its share of quacks, schemers, and subpar advice. It has also developed the reputation in some circles of being either cheesy or too "out there."

However, the truth remains: In many cases, you can, indeed, help yourself. And much of the time, you can use insights from the folks who have made their names working the self-help circuit— even those who are long gone. In many cases, life taught these authors what science and psychology would uncover years later. Countless studies have since backed up some of the insights of the very first self-help authors on numerous subjects, from gratitude to relationship-building.

But when it comes to knowing who to trust and what advice to take, things can get dicey. There are thousands of self-help titles out there, and over the years we've seen our share of snake oil that is printed, bound, and marketed to the public as the be all, end all way to cure what ails you. Even the most popular books on the subject take a sharp turn toward the nonsensical now and then. After all, there's no regulatory board or official set of standards when it comes to self-help literature. We find ourselves navigating the kooky alongside the credible.

How do you know how to proceed? That's where we come in.

Together we represent a pretty unique combination of perspectives.

Jim McCann is a successful entrepreneur, business leader, author, media personality, and philanthropist with a passion for helping people deliver smiles. His belief in the universal need for social connection led him to found 1-800-Flowers.com, Inc., one of the world's leading floral and gourmet gifting companies, and over the years, he's grown his operation with businesses and brands for gifting and celebratory occasions, from Harry & David® to The Popcorn Factory®. Jim is also deeply involved in philanthropy, including his work with Smile Farms, an organization he founded that provides meaningful agricultural jobs to adults with developmental disabilities.

George S. Everly Jr., PhD, FAPA is a leading psychologist and public health scholar who created an entire field of international practice in crisis intervention and human resilience. He founded the International Critical Incident Stress Foundation, an education and training organization dedicated to reducing the adverse effects of trauma and burnout in emergency services professionals. For forty-five years, he has had the honor of being a faculty member at some of the finest universities in the world, including Harvard and Johns Hopkins, where he currently teaches. There, he's assumed the role of educator, researcher, and even a career coach of sorts for his students. And his students have not always been the traditional sort. In addition to graduate students, he has taught entrepreneurs, business executives, physicians, nurses, attorneys, veterinarians, medical students, and even celebrities. He's also served as chief psychologist at Johns Hopkins Homewood Hospital Center and on numerous government teams, from the CDC to the US Department of Homeland Security.

We've each had big careers, but we bonded for the first time over something elemental to human existence: relationships.

We were deep in the throes of the COVID-19 pandemic when Jim read an article about the pandemic's impact on connection that George had published on *Psychology Today*'s website (see https://www.psychologytoday.com/intl/contributors/george-s-everly-jr-phd-abpp-faclp). Impressed by the piece, Jim wrote George a fan letter and asked him if he'd like to have a conversation. George wasn't quite sure what Jim wanted to talk about, but he agreed. Soon after our first chat, we became what Jim affectionately refers to as "COVID buddies," and the rest is history.

As our friendship grew, we realized that we shared numerous passions, including a desire to be the best version of ourselves, to help others do the same, to foster connections, and to fight the epidemic of loneliness that brought us together in the first place. We hope you'll use this book to do just that.

Together we've combined the scientific with the practical, drawing on research and real-world experience to identify the most influential and scientifically credible self-help books of the last century and share their core messages or recommendations. We've pulled from history, science, and psychology to tell you why these books are worth your attention. Most importantly, we tell you how to make them work for you. Consider this a one-stop shop for the best of the best in self-help. From harnessing the power of optimism to cultivating resilience and building a strong and supportive community, we cover the key tenets of building a better life for yourself.

How did we choose the books in these pages?

These selections don't represent an exhaustive list. Rather, we consider them among the most impactful by virtue of their sales, their originality, their potential for game-changing impact, or their scientific credibility. They're the books we believe everyone should read to help themselves (or someone else!) improve themselves, with the ultimate goal of becoming as happy and successful as possible.

How about the subjects we're covering?

That's where things got particularly scientific. We conducted a factor analysis of sorts, comparing the content of each of our books to determine which topics came up most frequently. Then we ran the list through the filter of our own experiences and those of historical figures, celebrities, and our most successful friends. Finally, we considered what science reveals about the habits, skills, and actions that are the greatest determinants of personal and professional success. We've taken all that information and distilled it into easy-to-read, action-oriented chapters, complete with the books, stories, and scientific concepts that explain why they're vital to your success.

In these pages, you'll find insights on optimism from the founder of the positive psychology movement, the scientific secrets that make "The Secret" worth knowing, the value of living to learn, success stories from historical figures (and even stars such as Amanda Kloots), and advice from us—two guys who have been around the block a time or two. If you close this book feeling more equipped to find success—whether you want to make it on your own terms, make the world a better place, or simply make it through the challenges ahead—and to be kind to yourself and others along the way, our job here is done.

PART 1

....

CHAPTER I

PLAY THE GLAD GAME: CHANGING YOUR LIFE BEGINS WITH CHANGING YOUR MIND

Faithless is he who says farewell when the road darkens.

—J. R. R. TOLKIEN

HAVE YOU EVER READ THE STORY OF POLLYANNA?

Pollyanna is the classic children's book written in 1913 by Eleanor H. Porter. It tells the story of Pollyanna Whittier, a young girl who goes to live with her stern Aunt Polly after the death of her parents. If ever there was an optimistic person, it's Pollyanna. Despite her tragic loss and subsequently being raised in a household where discipline is emphasized to the virtual exclusion of happiness, she remains joyful. In fact, Pollyanna is described as a young lady with an unquenchable thirst for the positive things in life.

That's why this fictional character continues to live on in so many hearts more than a century after Porter wrote her into being. Stop for just a moment and consider Pollyanna's description: *a young lady with an unquenchable thirst for the positive things in life*. Have you ever met someone like that? If you have, chances are you found them to have an almost magnetic appeal. Maybe you've even wished to have a similar pull.

How did Pollyanna remain so positive and optimistic amid so much hardship? Whenever bad things happened, she'd play a game that her father taught her called the "Just Being Glad Game." As Pollyanna explained, "The game was to just find something about everything to be glad about—no matter what 'twas."[3]

And that approach—that attitude—is why we're talking about Pollyanna now, all these years later.

In our introduction, we told you we're on a mission to make the journey of self-improvement as accessible and easy as possible. That necessitates answering a key question: *What determines who we are and who we will become?*

Ultimately, it's our attitudes: the way we approach and view the world. Perhaps the two most important attitudes we can possess are optimism and self-confidence. Our protagonist, Pollyanna, embodies the former.

Pollyanna's "Glad Game" reminds us of a more contemporary practice: the "attitude of gratitude." Today, the benefits of gratitude are well documented in science, psychology, and beyond. Imagine a world in which we actively, if not relentlessly, search for and find happiness in even the littlest of things—and make an effort to be grateful for them. We would likely see a wide range of benefits, individually and in society as a whole, from physiological improvements to increased productivity. But optimism is more than being "glad" or even grateful. Optimism is a sense of hopefulness. And it became Dr. Martin Seligman's life's work.

Dr. Seligman leapt to prominence in the field of clinical psychology with his groundbreaking research on what he called an "epidemic of depression." Through a series of experiments, he learned that pessimism and helplessness were often related to depression.

That's a tricky pill to swallow because science reveals that most of us are born pessimists. Negative experiences are encoded in the human brain ten times faster than are positive experiences, and it takes five positive comments to be as impactful as one negative comment.[4] We expect challenges, even failure. We focus on our weaknesses and dwell on our insecurities. That negative bent is a defense mechanism meant to protect us from the dangers of the outside world. Its defenses are so great that it takes months, if not years, to build a trusting relationship—meanwhile, it takes only seconds to destroy it!

But just because we're built this way doesn't mean it benefits us. Research suggests worry, or repetitive concern—another mechanism meant to help us avoid danger—may be the most toxic psychological process out there. The more you worry, the better you get at it.

Even trickier: Few, if any, of us think of ourselves as pessimists. We think of ourselves as realists. Thus, we become stuck.

But there's good news too. Dr. Seligman also found that helplessness is largely learned—we aren't born feeling incapable; our experiences make us feel that way. As his research continued, his focus switched from pessimism to its opposite: optimism. He found that optimistic people suffer depression less often than pessimistic people. Most importantly, he realized that, just as helplessness and depression could be acquired characteristics, optimism could also be learned.

That led Seligman to champion a new subfield of psychology in 1999, "positive psychology," which he built on the Greek traditions of *eudaimonia* (a good life), as espoused by Aristotle, and the humanistic psychology movement advanced by psychological bigwigs such as Abraham Maslow, Rollo May, Carl Rogers, Douglas McGregor, and Henry Murray. In many ways, positive psychology became the evidence behind some of the underlying principles of Napoleon Hill's *Think and Grow Rich* and other self-help heavyweights. Science and self-helpers agree that the first step toward transformation is awareness. We have to know what we need to change to make it happen. But if you can recognize and shift the beliefs you hold about yourself and the world, you can indeed become more optimistic.

Self-confidence is the natural corollary of optimism. It's the belief in your own abilities, that you can act as your own advocate and agent for change and live the life you've been hoping for.

WHY ARE OPTIMISM AND SELF-CONFIDENCE SO IMPORTANT?

Optimism serves as the first step on the path to self-improvement. It's the launchpad for becoming whomever you want to be and achieving whatever you wish to achieve. Optimistic people are less anxious, they get depressed less often, they are higher achievers, and they are physically healthier—it doesn't get any more important than that!

On the flip side, pessimistic people tend to have limited self-confidence. They perceive stressful events as unmanageable and are more likely to dwell on their perceived deficiencies, which generates increased stress and diminishes potential problem-solving energy, lowers aspirations, and weakens commitments. Pessimistic people are at higher risk for self-medication and substance misuse, and pessimists fail more often simply because they quit trying sooner than their optimistic counterparts. Where optimists see situational failures as stepping stones to success, pessimists see situational failures as confirmation of their expectations. For those reasons, and many more, making the effort to become more optimistic is some of the most important self-help work you can do.

Self-confidence is step two on that path. It gives you the guts to tackle tough challenges and overcome failure. Some have argued that self-confidence is the single most important determinant of your life's trajectory. It affects the actions you choose to pursue, the risks you're willing to take, how much effort you put into anything you go after, how long you will persevere, your resilience, whether your thoughts will be helpful or undermining, and how much stress and depression you will experience. In short, it determines what you will accomplish in your life! If you possess a high sense of self-confidence, you tend to be tenacious and find creative ways to achieve your goals when confronted by challenges and adversity.

Lead with Optimism

When it comes to the world's top leaders across industries—past and present—we'd venture to say that most of them are optimists. After all, pessimism can get in the way of trying new things and taking the chances that facilitate success. As Winston Churchill is purported to have said, "A pessimist sees the difficulty in every opportunity; an optimist sees the opportunity in every difficulty."

Warren Buffett, one of the most famous figures in finance, has said time and again that it's optimism—not money—that brokers happiness. And, as data scientist Michael Toth found, Buffett truly puts his money where his mouth is. Toth conducted a sentiment analysis (a technical term for what kids today might call a "vibe check") on the annual Berkshire Hathaway shareholder letters Buffett has written over a span of forty years. He found that the overwhelming majority of them were positive. Only five were negative, and those aligned with periods of recession in the US. "To me this communicates that even in negativity, Buffett is thinking about solutions and charting a path forward," Toth noted.[5]

And the handful of negative notes? They're actually an important element too. As Toth explained, "When things are going poorly, he's comfortable admitting that. . . . People who are confident that they will succeed and equally confident that success won't come easily put in more effort, plan how to deal with problems before they arise, and persist longer in the face of difficulty."[6]

Jim's friend and business partner Bob Diamond, an American banker and former chief executive officer of Barclays, is a lifelong optimist—so much so that his nickname at work is "Bobtimist." His optimism is one of his most attractive qualities and a key component of his success. (According to his Wikipedia description, "Robert Edward Diamond Jr. is an American banker and former chief executive officer of Barclays plc. In 2010, he became its president and deputy group chief executive; in January 2011, he succeeded John Varley as group chief executive of Barclays.")

But from time to time, Bob will say, "I hope I'm not just being a Bobtimist here." He's self-aware enough to understand

the occasional challenges of such an orientation—that unbridled
optimism can cloud one's vision. It's why he balances his approach
with a COO, CFO, and partners who are true realists (not pessimists) and thus help him understand the actual probabilities of his
organization's activities.

Cultivating a more optimistic outlook will take you far, but
judicious pessimism has its place. Anticipating risks and threats
to success can be prudent—it's why so many of us are pessimistic
to begin with! Optimism should never blind us to the sometimes-
unpleasant realities of the world in which we live. What it should
do is keep those realities from overwhelming us so that we can
move beyond them. For Bob, surrounding himself with people
who can play that role means he can reach for the stars without
losing his head in the clouds. He expects everything will work out,
and more often than not, it does. Meanwhile, his team keeps his
optimistic tendencies in check.

Train Your Brain
What if you're not an optimist by nature?

Fortunately, optimism is a gift you can give yourself. Science
tells us that you can train your brain using the biological mechanism of neuroplasticity: the brain's ability to change. A type of
brain scan called the MRI has shown that it is possible to rewire
the brain to be more optimistic. Perhaps the multi-hyphenate and
unequivocally successful Oprah Winfrey said it best: "The greatest
discovery of all time is that a person can change his future by
merely changing his attitude." It doesn't require a fancy machine
or even a therapist; consistent practice is all you need. And when
you do take on a glass-half-full perspective, you'll begin to see
opportunity everywhere you look. George is proof.

George's dad was a finance guy who thought about the world in terms of worst-case scenarios, a trait he passed on to George. In fact, considering the worst-case scenario became the subject of George's work: he made a career—and helped create an entire field—out of studying disasters and crises and their effects on mental health and human behavior. As a result of personally studying disasters such as Hurricane Katrina, Three Mile Island, the World Trade Center disaster of September 11, the Gulf War, the Fukushima Daiichi nuclear disaster, the SARS pandemic in Hong Kong, the H1N1 pandemic in Singapore, the COVID-19 pandemic here in the United States, and numerous other disasters in thirty-nine countries over time, something shifted. He noticed that while adversity and even disasters could be tragic, there were some who arose from adversity, trauma, and disaster stronger than ever before, like the fabled phoenix. From that point on he focused on identifying the sources of human strength and resilience. In the aggregate, George's experience represented a most unique perspective and an opportunity to identify that which gives rise to resilience, heroism, and growth. Two of the most important factors he repeatedly saw were optimism and a vision for the future. These allow us to arise from the ashes of adversity and despair bigger, better, bolder, and stronger than ever before.

A heroine you probably learned about in primary school also believed in tapping into the benefits of learned optimism. Helen Keller became the first deaf and blind person to earn a bachelor of arts degree, and she went on to become a disability rights advocate, activist, and author—penning fourteen books in addition to speeches and essays. Her story is one of optimism and triumph. But she wasn't born an optimist. In one piece, "Optimism: An

Essay," Keller explains that she understood optimism as a mindset cultivated over time. She writes, "The struggle which evil necessitates is one of the greatest blessings. It makes us strong, patient, helpful men and women. It lets us into the soul of things and teaches us that although the world is full of suffering, it is full also of the overcoming of it."[7]

Just as Keller noted, the most powerful way to increase your own self-confidence, self-determination, and optimism is with repetition. If you weren't born optimistic, the way Pollyanna was, you've got to practice being optimistic. And to do that, you must embrace the challenges that come your way. Challenge helps us exercise our optimism muscle; and we grow psychologically stronger with each rep.

Meanwhile, avoiding the possibility of rejection and failure deprives us of the chance to grow. But pick your battles carefully at first. Go for increasingly difficult challenges so that success can build on itself. When tasks are large, break them down into manageable bites and take them one at a time.

Keep in mind, too, that your thoughts can literally create success or failure. That's because only you can define success for yourself. As such, your objective successes don't increase your optimism if you perceive your success as failure. On the other hand, if you view a "failure" as a necessary stepping stone on the way to your goal, you can consider it a success. Take the military leader who, when forced to retreat on the battlefield, emphatically responded that he did not retreat; he merely chose to advance in another direction.

Look to Others

Other ways to increase optimism and self-confidence? Observation and vicarious experiences. That is, if you watch someone similar to you succeed at something, you're more likely to be optimistic about your own ability to do so—and that much closer to making it happen. An older sibling, an inspiring friend, or even a celebrity with a backstory similar to your own can give you the confidence to pursue a new challenge or opportunity or to follow a path you've been too nervous to take.

You can also enhance your own optimism and self-confidence by seeking encouragement from others. Constructive criticism, compliments, coaching, and mentorship build self-confidence, along with the sense that everything will turn out OK.

But this strategy comes with a couple of caveats. First, the source of encouragement must be credible. This isn't someone who merely tells you what they think you want to hear—your mother, who would reassure you that you can definitely make it as a Major League Baseball player even if you have Tee-ball level skills, for instance. But the high school coach who's seen you play and believes you have what it takes to make it to the big leagues? That's fair game.

It's also important to note that you can't just take the compliments and leave behind the constructive criticism; you must be willing to accept both. Don't get defensive in the face of a thoughtful critique (and note: that may take some practice too). By the same token, you should *never* dismiss a sincere compliment. Let it boost your confidence so you can tackle the additional challenges that come your way.

Get Ahold of Yourself

With a plan for tackling challenges, it's time to consider a crucial skill: self-control. You may have heard of the Marshmallow Test, one of the most famous psychological studies of all time. In the '60s and '70s, clinical psychologist Walter Mischel placed a single treat in front of children between three and five years old and told them that if they could wait several minutes to eat it—until a researcher left the room and returned—they could have two treats.

Those treats weren't trivial: whether or not they could wait seemed to predict how successful the children would be over the course of their lives—in school and beyond. Since then, the Marshmallow Test has been used to explain the value of self-control when it comes to performance and, ultimately, happiness.

How many times have you reacted emotionally or impulsively, particularly when there's a lot on the line, and regretted it later—often instantly? It's difficult, if not impossible, to feel good about the future when you keep getting in your own way.

Meanwhile, when you're in control of your behavior, you're in control of your life. You can be optimistic about how things will unfold because you trust yourself to do what's necessary in any circumstance. That's powerful stuff.

Now, what do the self-help books say about the role of optimism and self-confidence in one's life?

THE BEST SELF-HELP BOOKS ON OPTIMISM AND SELF-CONFIDENCE

Think and Grow Rich by Napoleon Hill

Self-help authors have been touting the benefits of optimism and self-confidence for generations. Napoleon Hill published one of the earliest self-improvement books, *Think and Grow Rich*, back in 1937. Hill wrote the book at the end of the Great Depression, when people were hungry for an economic renaissance—both personal and societal. The book is based on Hill's study of people who had grown great personal fortunes, most notably Henry Ford, Andrew Carnegie, and Thomas Edison.

Think and Grow Rich appealed to self-starters. It gave them hope that, with little more than their thoughts, they could build a better life for themselves. But the text isn't without its faults.

The book was initially received with some skepticism, and later investigations into Hill's life suggest a wayward past—and that he may have never met any of the industry giants he claimed to have interviewed for the book. There are certainly some cringeworthy sections of *Think and Grow Rich*, and some sentiments haven't aged very well. But, nearly a century later, *Think and Grow Rich* stands as the Rosetta Stone of self-help texts, having sold tens of millions of copies. Experts agree that, regardless of whether Hill's anecdotes were fact or fiction, the principles are psychologically and spiritually sound. Essentially, the way we think about the world and ourselves has a tremendous impact on how our lives turn out.

With that in mind, Hill's four-step Self-Confidence Formula is worth holding on to:

- **Trust in your talents:** Believe that you have the ability to achieve your life's purpose. When you do, you're that much closer to making it happen.
- **Know thyself:** If you understand the way you think—and the thoughts that dominate your mind—you can turn your dreams into reality, thriving and flourishing on your own terms.

- **Focus on the future:** Spend thirty minutes a day concentrating on the person you want to become, and you can't help but take on some of those traits.
- **Write it down:** Write a description of your life's "definite chief aim" and never stop trying to achieve it. Studies show that when you put pen to paper and jot down your goals, you're much more likely to meet them.

The Power of Positive Thinking by Norman Vincent Peale

Since its publication in 1952, Norman Vincent Peale's *The Power of Positive Thinking* has sold over fifteen million copies worldwide, making it one of the most referenced guides on maintaining optimism through life's peaks and valleys. In it, Peale teaches readers that life can be full of joy and peace if careful, daily attention is paid to maintaining an optimistic outlook and a healthy mind. The crux of Peale's theory is that every individual has the ability to overcome obstacles through self-belief, mental fortitude, and faith—as informed by the author's experience as a minister. He writes, "If happiness is determined by our thoughts, it is necessary to drive off the thoughts which make for depression and discouragement." In other words, keep accentuating the positive and do your best to drop the negative. Sounds like a lesson on engaging the benefits of neuroplasticity to us.

Learned Optimism: How to Change Your Mind and Your Life by Dr. Martin Seligman

While *Learned Optimism* isn't a self-help book in the traditional sense, it's chock-full of helpful advice on becoming a true optimist.

What's the meat of Marty's message? He offers two vital insights on becoming more optimistic and self-confident: explanatory styles and the ABCDE of learned optimism. Consider them your prescription and treatment, respectively.

Explanatory styles are the ways we interpret and relate to the world around us. When it comes to explanatory styles, it turns out that optimists and pessimists do things differently. Seligman uses the 3Ps (Permanence, Pervasiveness, and Personal Control) to explain the key differences in how pessimists and optimists think:

1. **Permanence: Pessimists believe their problems are chronic, while optimists see problems as temporary.**

2. **Pervasiveness: Pessimists see the stuff that plagues them as pervasive, infiltrating all aspects of their life.** Optimists see them as being specific and limited in scope.

3. **Personal Control: Pessimists blame themselves for most of those problems—even the ones they didn't really create.** Worse, they often waste time trying to change people and things over which they have no control, resulting in frustration, bitterness, and despair. Optimists recognize that many of the things that go wrong are beyond their control. That helps them play the Glad Game rather than the Blame Game.

The good news: you can shift from pessimist to optimist by focusing on the 3Ps. The ABCDE formula can help you along the way. Think of it as a way to analyze the challenges you're experiencing and to figure out a constructive way forward. Let's walk through the ABCDE model.

- **A—Adversity:** In this step, you identify the people or situations that most often cause you to think pessimistically or lose your self-confidence.

- **B—Belief:** What are you telling yourself about the situation? What "self-talk" dialogue are you having about the cause of your problems?

  Consider your explanatory style here too. Does your problem seem like it will last forever? Does it feel like it will affect every part of your life? Are you blaming yourself for the issue at hand, even if it's not your doing? Finally, how do you imagine it will all play out? Are you catastrophizing—assuming the worst-possible outcome? If the answer to any of these is yes, you've got some work to do.
- **C—Consequences:** Here, you identify how those beliefs have changed how you feel (for example, are you feeling depressed or depleted?) and how you act (are you irritable, angry, avoidant, sleeping more, eating more?).
- **D—Dispute:** In this step, you search for reasonable and realistic ways to dispute or contradict either the cause or the outcome of the adversity.
- **E—Energize:** This is when you make a plan for change.

Research suggests that through the use of the principles and practices described in *Learned Optimism*, you can become more confident and happier. But as you can see, it's not a passive process. You've got to commit to making the change and to putting in the work necessary to make it stick. Tenacious practice is key. So is a willingness to see the light, even in the darkest of times—as television personality, dancer, and fitness entrepreneur Amanda Kloots knows all too well.

PLAYING THE GLAD GAME
WITH AMANDA KLOOTS

Years of personal and professional experience have taught us that real stories can help bring the insights we're sharing to life. Amanda Kloots's story can teach us important lessons on optimism and self-confidence. Optimism helped Amanda realize her dream, even amid unlikely circumstances and devastating tragedy. She has proved that we can always listen to the melodies of our loved ones, even when their songs have ended.

For Amanda, her optimism was combined with, as she explained, "A lot of hard work. A lot of determination. A lot of lessons. A lot of not giving up."

Amanda grew up in Canton, Ohio. Her father was an insurance salesman and her mother stayed home to take care of Amanda and her four siblings. It was a Norman Rockwell painting of an American existence: she and her siblings spent long afternoons biking through the neighborhood with their friends, and their father would whistle when it was time to come home for dinner—just after the streetlights flickered on.

But in middle school, Amanda's world began to open up. She was chosen to be one of the children in the local high school's production of *Fiddler on the Roof.* Singing the opening number, "Tradition," her arms rose above her head and she realized, *I want to do this for the rest of my life.* She was officially in love with musical theater.

As high school graduation neared, she begged her parents to send her to a program that would help her get to Broadway—a musical theater conservatory or a great college with a musical theater program.

Ultimately they agreed, letting her move to New York City at eighteen to attend a conservatory and pursue her dreams.

"It's a hard life.... You're competing against people that are just as talented, if not more talented, than you. Every single day, you're getting told 'no.' You have to have the thickest skin. You have to be really self-confident and have a lot of self-esteem, and you have to be willing to keep working, because the work never stops," she said.

Amanda went on to become a Rockette and a Broadway performer. She met Nick Cordero, an actor, when they were both cast in the show *Bullets over Broadway*. They married in September of 2017 and had their son, Elvis, in June of 2019. Soon after, they moved to Los Angeles so that Nick could pursue television acting and music production. And then the world went a little cockeyed on her—as it does to us all.

The COVID-19 pandemic hit. In late March of 2020, Nick went into the hospital with what the couple thought was pneumonia and what would later be diagnosed as COVID-19. Amanda began sharing her journey with her fifty thousand Instagram followers. Every day, she shared daily "AK! Positive Thought of the Day" posts and hosted a three-o'clock sing-along to one of Nick's original songs, "Live Your Life," in hopes that the collective energy would help heal her husband.

"People really needed people during the pandemic. They needed a community, they needed something to go to, something to believe in," she said. In awe of her strength and positivity, and in search of some optimism of their own, hundreds of thousands of people began following her journey on Instagram. "That whole army that was created at that time, I'll never forget it. It was a lifeline for me. It was such a support system, and it still is," Amanda said.

Nick died of complications from COVID-19 after more than ninety days in the hospital. But even in the face of the worst-possible tragedy, Amanda stayed optimistic. As Susan Stroman, a theater director, choreographer, and colleague explained, "Amanda is a very positive person. In dire times, she will try to bring something into being with the force of her positivity." That positivity continued to galvanize her community.

In the six months following Nick's death, Amanda wrote a *New York Times* bestselling book, *Live Your Life: My Story of Loving and Losing Nick Cordero*, about the ordeal, which she is adapting into a movie. She went on to be a contestant on *Dancing with the Stars*. "On tour with *Dancing with the Stars*, so many people would come out to see me and say hello and tell me they followed my story from back when I first started my fitness business. It's beautiful. It's really cool to see how social media can make such an impact," she told Jim. A few months later, she became a cohost of the Emmy Award–winning daytime talk show, *The Talk*.

Amanda's career continues to flourish. She wrote and will be starring in a Christmas movie that will air on CBS. She also has a children's book in the works, in addition to parenting her young son, Elvis. "Losing somebody that you love at forty-one years old, it made me appreciate life. It made me work harder in my life. It made me hug people longer, kiss people goodbye, say I love you more, go for my dreams even more than I would already go for my dreams," Amanda said.

"If you would have asked me five years ago, 'Do you think that you will be a talk show host with a *New York Times* bestselling book and writing a screenplay from it?' I would have laughed in your face. I don't know what the world holds, and I don't know if I ever want to try to guess, because I feel like life is so full of surprises and the twists and turns are so unexpected. I'm just trying to be very present in the day and be excited about what the future holds.

"I always say, 'Pick one thing—one flower—a day that you're grateful for, and at the end of the week you'll have a beautiful bouquet.'" We think that's advice worth taking to heart.

LODESTAR

Not a born optimist? That's OK! With a little effort, you'll be playing the Glad Game in no time. Keep the following key points in mind:

- **Repetition is the key to neuroplasticity.** You can give yourself the gift of optimism, regardless of your current thinking patterns or situation. It all comes down to repetition. Work on being an optimist by purposefully looking for the opportunity in all situations, and you'll ultimately rewire your brain to become one.

- **Remember your 3Ps (and ABCDEs).** If it seems like all that optimistic thinking is easier said than done, channel the father of positive psychology: Dr. Martin Seligman. To turn the tables on a pessimistic perspective, consider Dr. Seligman's 3Ps of Permanence, Pervasiveness, and Personal Control as well as his ABCDE formula of Adversity, Belief, Consequences, Dispute, and Energize, and use them to flip the switch.

- **You don't have to go it alone.** The Glad Game can truly improve the quality of your life, but you don't have to play it all by yourself. Looking to others for inspiration and encouragement can help you succeed in achieving an optimistic outlook, along with goals of all sizes.

....

CHAPTER 2

BELIEVE AND YOU WILL RECEIVE: HARNESSING THE POWER OF PROPHECY

The ultimate function of prophecy is not to tell the future, but to make it.

—W. WARREN WAGAR

WHAT IF YOU COULD BUILD THE LIFE YOU'VE ALWAYS DREAMED OF using just your mind?

Many self-help authors tell you that you can do just that. It may sound unlikely, but with a little digging, you'll find that science and human experience support their claims.

We're talking about the self-fulfilling prophecy, the basis of books such as *The Secret* and *The Law of Attraction*. It starts with the foundational elements of self-improvement that we just discussed: optimism and self-confidence. We think of optimism as the inclination to be positive and hopeful. Self-confidence is the functional extension of optimism. It's the belief that you can successfully act on your own behalf, that you can be an agent of change in your life and—within reason—the director of your own destiny.

The notion of "prophecy" isn't a new concept; in fact, it may be as old as humanity itself. You'll find it throughout Greek mythology and in the Old Testament. The word comes from the Greek *prophēteia*, which means the "gift of interpreting the will of the gods." Back in the day, seers—or prophets—would predict the will of deities and use those insights to set expectations for the future.

The seer's announcement of the prophecy was a passive prediction in the sense that they were just the messengers. But the concept of the self-fulfilling prophecy holds that it's possible to take your fate into your own hands. Armed with active expectation, prophecy can become reality. Where strength of mind persists, destiny will often follow.

The self-fulfilling prophecy's academic roots go back to 1928, when William Isaac Thomas and Dorothy Swaine Thomas came up with the aptly named Thomas theorem. It states that "if we imagine situations to be real, they are real in their consequences." But the concept wouldn't get its name until 1948, when sociologist Robert Merton described it in a paper titled "The Self-Fulfilling Prophecy." In it, he wrote, "Were the Thomas theorem and its implications more widely known, more men would understand more of the workings of our society." Or, as industrialist Henry Ford famously said, "Whether you think you can or you can't, you are right."

Shakespeare's play *Macbeth* is a famous literary example of the darker side of the self-fulfilling prophecy. Three witches greet the Scottish general Macbeth with a prophecy that he shall someday be king. Fueled by their words and the greed of his wife, Lady Macbeth, the prophecy becomes an expectation that he will actually become king of Scotland. The expectation becomes a quest that overwhelms his usual dutiful and honorable self, emerging in unscrupulous and murderous ways.

The witches' prophecy ultimately comes true: Macbeth indeed becomes king. But this isn't the "happily ever after" Macbeth was anticipating. He's eventually killed to avenge the murders he committed in his journey to take and retain the throne. It doesn't have to be all doom and gloom, though—particularly when you harness the power of the self-fulfilling prophecy for good.

Future Shock author Alvin Toffler once wrote, "If we do not learn from history, we shall be compelled to relive it. True. But if we do not change the future, we shall be compelled to endure it. And that could be worse." Author William Arthur Ward took that notion, personalized it, and added a positive spin: "If you can imagine it, you can achieve it. If you can dream it, you can become it."

WHY IS SELF-FULFILLING PROPHECY SO IMPORTANT?

Essentially, self-fulfilling prophecy enables you to change the future for the better. It can help you chart your life's trajectory or allow you to realize your renaissance. That is, if you believe it can. And it most definitely behooves you to believe it.

If You Can See It, You Can Be It

Over the years, people have asked Jim if he ever imagined his first flower shop becoming a big company. The answer is yes, he did imagine it. He is a big believer in daydreaming. He has always felt that when you create the fiction of what something might look like, you're much more likely to achieve it. Science agrees. The central nervous system is incapable of telling the difference between fantasy and reality. The more you imagine something, the more the brain rewires itself to achieve that particular outcome through neuroplasticity and the more real that fantasy becomes.

Back in the day, George put that process to the test. He was a consultant to Olympic weightlifters, and to help those weightlifters improve their performances he employed visualization.

The bench press wasn't an Olympic event, but it was a very well controlled exercise, and that meant George could use it to study the impact of visualization on athletes' performance. He told the athletes to think about a neutral image, getting it as crisp and clear as possible in their mind. Then, he would take the standard weight, load it onto the bar, put it on their chests, and see how many repetitions they could do, controlling for all other factors. Next, he asked them to visualize doing the exercise as well as possible, lifting the weight with ease. With that image loaded into their minds, they were able to improve their performance significantly.

The exercise led to the realization that when weightlifters reach what appears to be their maximum weight, it's psychological, not physical. Ultimately, it's the mind—not the body—that pushes one past a particular threshold. With that in mind, don't hesitate to see the version of you that you wish to be in the world.

Of course, visualization has its limitations: Jim's dating life didn't quite match up with the one he imagined, and there are a lot of unfulfilled, unhappy, unsuccessful people out there who are very good at imagining a bigger, brighter future for themselves. What's the differentiating factor between unsuccessful people with a rich fantasy life and the ones who do big things? The willingness to do something about it. What you think about matters, but what you *do* makes all the difference.

Before Jim's success with 1-800-Flowers, the first decade or so in business was a series of failures—but without a willingness to fall down. He could suffer those failures because he could see a successful image of the future, and he knew it would take trial and error to get to that better place. Plus, he felt he had no choice but to keep going; if he stopped, that would be the true failure. Meanwhile, if he pressed on, there was a chance he could find the right path.

One of George's closest friends showed a similar brand of persistence. The man, a guy we'll call Tom, went to business school with George, and at the end of the program, they both decided they'd continue their schooling. Both applied to PhD programs, but Tom received rejection after rejection. He took the LSAT in an attempt to go to law school but got the lowest score on record. One night, about a year later, George went to his house for dinner. Tom had a manila envelope on the table—about an inch thick.

"What's that?" George asked.

"It's all my rejection letters from postgrad programs," he replied.

"What are you saving 'em for?"

"Well, when I get my PhD, I'm gonna send them all invitations to my graduation."

He was making progress toward that goal. When he couldn't get into a graduate program through the front door, he found an alternative route. A local university offered people the opportunity to take one-off courses as a special student. Unlike many institutions, there was no limit to the number of special student courses one could take. So Tom began going through the doctoral program in psychology as a nonmatriculated student. When he was three courses short of completing the program, he applied for admission. At that point, he had done quite well, and the school essentially had to let him in. Ultimately, he graduated at the top of his class, and that manila folder of rejection letters came in quite handy.

Today, he's a successful businessperson by any standard. The decision to do something is what got him there.

Dress for the Job You Want, Not the Job You Have

Another factor to take into account when harnessing the power of prophecy? Others' impressions of you.

In 1975, John Molloy penned the bestselling book *Dress for Success*. Based on the title, you might think it was a book about clothing styles. In reality, it was a game-changing lesson about the self-fulfilling prophecy.

Dress for Success cites research on how clothing affects peoples' opinions of the wearer, validating what we already knew: we judge people based on the way they dress. We treat people differently based on what they're wearing too. But don't fret. You can use this knowledge to your advantage.

You can create a self-fulfilling prophecy by dressing the way you wish to be perceived. It's the old, "Dress for the job you want, not the job you have," backed by data. The actor John Travolta once said that one of the keys to a successful audition was to dress as if you already have the part. Doing that makes it easier for people to envision you in the role. As it turns out, that's a scientific truth.

The power of the self-fulfilling prophecy goes beyond what you wear. Research on interpersonal attraction indicates that people who are considered physically attractive are assessed more positively overall than those who are seen as less physically attractive. But wait, studies on attractiveness reveal an amazing fact: if people believe they are physically attractive, they are more likely to be *seen* and *treated* as if they really are! Beauty is in the eye of the beholder, but you have the power to influence what they see.

Fake It 'til You Make It

When it comes to influencing others, we can take a lesson from Muhammad Ali, perhaps the greatest heavyweight boxer of all time. Ali knew he was a good boxer—a great boxer, even—but he wanted to be known as "the greatest." Rather than waiting to become the greatest, and then for people to buy into the idea, he started referring to himself that way. He did it relentlessly. And lo and behold, people began thinking of him as such.

Ali later admitted, "I am the greatest. I said that even before I knew I was. I figured that if I said it enough, I would convince the world that I was really the greatest." It worked—for him. In truth, he began to believe it, and truly act like the greatest, only when others started saying it back to him. He faked it until he made it.

The benefits of the self-fulfilling prophecy aren't just available to people hoping to make it in Hollywood or sports. Anyone can use it to achieve their dreams.

A young woman found herself plagued with the same kind of worries when she went away to college at a top university. She was intimidated by her classmates and the environment itself. She told her father about her concerns. "I go to a party and everybody's smarter than I am," she said.

Though he knew that it would just take time for her to get up to speed and feel comfortable, her father could tell those feelings were eroding her confidence. He gave her some advice.

"The first thing you have to keep in mind is that everyone's favorite subject is themselves. So be a good listener, learn how to ask questions. You may meet a PhD student in quantum physics, and you may not even know how to *spell* quantum physics—let alone anything about it. That's OK. Say, 'Well, that sounds fascinating. Tell me about it.' It's not like there's going to be a quiz afterward. As people become comfortable sharing a part of their lives with you, they'll naturally assume that you understand them. In turn, you *will* come to understand them."

He went on to tell her about a principle called the Halo Effect. It states that, if people believe you are successful at something, they will transfer that belief into expectations of success. That includes giving you credit for successes you haven't earned yet. They'll even forgive your mistakes. And ultimately, they'll give you more opportunities than they would give someone else. Just ask Muhammad Ali.

Despite an initial challenge of self-confidence, her belief in herself blossomed, and four years later that young woman graduated on the dean's list from Harvard University.

Play Host

What if anxiety is getting in the way of convincing others—or
yourself—what you're capable of? Play host.

Jim learned early on that the best way to overcome shyness is
to act like a host. So it wasn't an accident that he found himself
working in retail as a kid; it forced him to interact with the public.
And it wasn't a mistake that he wound up working as a bartender
later on; it put him in the center of the action and gave him a
reason to be there. When he had kids, he began telling them how
to overcome their shyness. "Look for someone else who's obviously
struggling and help them with their issue," he said. It's something
he continues to do to this day—the host mentality has become a
self-fulfilling prophecy, just a part of who he is.

In fact, he had the opportunity to unleash it just the other day.
He was invited to an event hosted by Jamie Dimon, the chairman
and CEO of JP Morgan Chase. It's part of a tradition that Jamie
and his team started some years ago. They take a bus tour of a
different region of the country each August. They visit customers
at breakfasts, lunches, and dinners; hold interactive talks; and visit
with local branch tellers over donuts and coffee.

Jim and Jamie have known each other for twenty-five years.
They both grew up in Queens, though in different neighborhoods.
Jim has always enjoyed spending time with Jamie and admires
his talent in making very complicated things sound simple: "Oh,
inflation, it's this and this and that. To combat it, you just do
that, and boom, fixed." That means his Q&A sessions are always
entertaining.

At the event Jim attended—at a restaurant in the center of
Long Island—Jim picked up his name tag and headed for his
table. His seatmate was a young man with whom he'd done some

business, an accomplished emergency room doc who cocreated a highly successful walk-in urgent care clinic with over a hundred locations in the New York area. The man had since built several other successful companies. Jamie Dimon himself would be sitting across from them.

"Jim," his seatmate said, "I'm so nervous about sitting so close to Jamie, I can barely speak."

The woman on the other side of him—an executive at a leading beauty brand—chimed in. "Me too! My knees are shaking."

Just then, Jamie walked in wearing a pair of blue jeans and a black polo shirt. The room got quiet and then broke into applause. Jim worried his poor seatmate would faint. When it was time for Jamie to take his seat, Jim waved him over, and Jamie responded by putting him in a friendly headlock.

"Jeez, I haven't seen you in like six months," Jamie said. "What's going on?"

The banter relaxed the table a bit, as the nervous guests began to see that the legendary Jamie Dimon was just a regular guy.

"Jamie," Jim said, "let me introduce you to a couple of people around the table. This is David, a very accomplished physician. He's an emergency room guy, and I partnered with him when he created his first company."

Jamie smiled and smacked David on the back, "So what the hell have you done so far today?" he said.

Then Jim introduced him to the woman at the table next. "She's moving to Forest Hills next month when she gets married, just a few blocks from where you grew up in that ritzy-ditsy neighborhood."

"Oh, it wasn't so ritzy-ditsy," Jamie replied. "You keep saying that!"

After the event, the man and woman who had been nervous to meet Jamie came up to Jim. "Thank you. You turned what could've been a scary experience into something fun," they told him.

The next morning, Jamie wrote Jim a quick note, "Great to see you. I hope I didn't make you uncomfortable with that exchange."

He hadn't. Jamie is a master at making people feel comfortable. As someone of his stature—one of the most recognized people in the country, maybe in the world—he has to be. It's part of why he wears jeans and a polo shirt to events (regular guy clothes), visits with bank tellers over crullers and bear claws, and acts as if he's known you forever. Jamie knows the secret Jim's been sharing for as long as he can remember: acting as a host is a great way to get over your own anxieties and to create an environment that's more fun for everyone. Before you know it, you'll be the host you aspired to be—even if you had to fake it the first few times.

LESSONS FROM THE BEST SELF-HELP BOOKS ON THE SELF-FULFILLING PROPHECY

The Secret by Rhonda Byrne

When Rhonda Byrne set out to produce a film on the law of attraction in 2004, she had no budget and no plan of attack. All she knew was that she believed it would be so, and it would change her life and the lives of many others. Similar to Napoleon Hill's *Think and Grow Rich*, *The Secret* shares the stories of some of history's most successful people—including Winston Churchill, Abraham Lincoln, and Ludwig van Beethoven—as evidence of its effectiveness.

The film—and the 2006 book of the same name—took the world by storm, selling over thirty million copies in fifty different languages. Byrne became a household name, appearing on talk shows like *Oprah* and landing on *TIME* magazine's Top 100 Most Influential People list in 2007.

So, what's the, you know, secret of *The Secret?*

Byrne breaks it down into three simple steps: Ask, Believe, and Receive.

- **Ask.** The first step involves asking the capital-U Universe for anything you desire, which Byrne compares to ordering from an infinite cosmic menu. According to Byrne, since the Universe does not have a concept of size, asking for one dollar or a million of them makes no difference—the sky's the limit. While we can't confirm if that's true or not, we do know that imagining a particular outcome can help plant the seeds necessary to achieve it.

  The trick here is to be specific, just as George's Olympic weightlifting team was when they were at the bench press.

- **Believe.** From there, you must have the faith that you have the power to control your own destiny and that all things will come to you in good time if you believe that to be true. You have to *know* that things will turn out the way you want. Byrne holds that when you believe, the Universe will too. Studies haven't garnered insights from the Universe itself, but—as you'll remember—they have shown that your conviction has the power to sway others' opinions.

- **Receive.** The last step is simple: ultimately, you'll receive what you want. That doesn't necessarily mean you won't have to take any action. Rather, Byrne suggests that your path will be cleared by hurdles, and all the elements out of your control will fall into place. It's your expectation for success and the effort that flows from that belief that determine whether you achieve your goals or not.

The Law of Attraction by Esther and Jerry Hicks

Decades before Rhonda Byrne released *The Secret*, Esther and Jerry Hicks shared their teachings on how the Universe conspires to fulfill whatever destiny you believe to be truly yours.

The Hickses' method for obtaining the insights they share in *The Law of Attraction* is admittedly a little out there—they claim the principles are translated from nonphysical entities that speak to them from the beyond—but wherever they come from, they seem to work. Further, we can find a scientific basis for some of their strategies (more on that in a moment).

Which concepts from the book are worth pocketing for future use?

- **Mind Your Frequency.** The Hickses' take on frequencies is particularly sound. One thing we know to be true: thoughts are composed of energy, and different thoughts vibrate at different frequencies (we know this because we can physically measure brain waves using tools such as an EEG).

    We also know that energy tends to be attracted to other energy of the same frequency. It's this concept that produces the sitar's droning sounds—when a main string is plucked, the neighboring strings vibrate along with it at the same frequency; these are called sympathetic strings. It stands to reason, then, that whatever the frequency of the thoughts you put out into the Universe, a similar energy will be returned to you.

To change your frequency, the Hickses recommend using positive affirmations that condition your mind to believe not only that positive things are coming your way but also that they're already in your orbit. These might look like positive self-talk or *I am* statements—phrases to reassure yourself that you're up to the task at hand.

- **Accentuate the Positive.** According to our self-fulfilling prophecy philosophers, the fact that you're a magnet for everything that comes into your life can be beneficial or disastrous. Of course, no one consciously attracts negative things into their lives, but it's easy to slip into negative self-talk.

  Ever notice that when your friend is complaining about their day, or a coworker is criticizing your boss, you feel the urge to join in? That's vibration-matching in action. And when you broadcast those negative thoughts, you fall into a pattern of thinking them (hello, neuroplasticity!). Your day will become as bad as your friend's, and anything your boss assigns you will feel frustrating and unnecessary.

  As such, you must learn to shape your thoughts and only put out what you wish to receive. In short, think positive thoughts and you'll eventually become the optimist you wish to be (you'll also be that much closer to achieving your best-laid plans).

Chicken Soup for the Soul by Jack Canfield and Mark Victor Hansen

Jack Canfield, *Chicken Soup for the Soul*'s cocreator, embodies the power of the self-fulfilling prophecy. Today, the *Chicken Soup for the Soul* series includes over 250 titles, has been published in more than forty languages, and has sold over five hundred million copies. But before that, a young Jack began his career as a high school teacher in Chicago. His meager teacher's salary barely covered the cost of city living, and he set out to change that.

His theory was that if he set a goal and pursued it with enough ferocity, it could be willed into being. Jack decided then that he would make $100,000. So, he drew up a picture of the dream sum and taped it to the ceiling above his bed. Vowing to do anything necessary to achieve his goal, he ended the year having earned $97,000—a lot more than the teaching job paid!

What began with a single slip of paper became Canfield's reality. Rather than simply fantasizing about his future, he created it through expectation and calculated daily pursuit.

In the decades since, Jack has held fast to these tenets as a global thought leader and motivational speaker—and even holds a Guinness World Record for having seven books on the *New York Times* bestseller list at the same time. His net worth currently stands at $50 million.

This thinking plays out in the first installment of *Chicken Soup for the Soul*, which includes 101 stories meant to cultivate hope and inspiration. There are numerous stories that highlight the power of the self-fulfilling prophecy, including a piece by Virginia Satir, an American author and psychotherapist.

To answer a fifteen-year-old's question, "How can I prepare myself for a fulfilling life?" Virginia responded, "I own me and therefore I can engineer me." When living intentionally and in alignment with what we seek, our thoughts (both those that seem fantastical *and* those that seem achievable) become reality. Entrepreneur and racing enthusiast Emmet Keeffe is a perfect example.

RACING TOWARD THE FUTURE YOU
WANT WITH EMMET KEEFFE

Emmet Keeffe has transformed multiple dreams into reality by harnessing the power of the self-fulfilling prophecy. They weren't small dreams either. In fact, Emmet firmly believes that if someone doesn't laugh when you share your goals for the future, they're not big enough. And his story is proof of that.

Emmet always knew he wanted to start his own company, but he spent the first ten years of his career in sales. First, it was copiers. Then it was health-care imaging equipment for hospitals, then hardware, then software. That didn't stop him from putting his long-term aspirations out there, though. On every single sales call, the first thing he'd say was, "Hi, my name's Emmet Keeffe, and I want to start my own business. Do you have any ideas for me?"

He was trying to find an answer to his question first and foremost. But he didn't want to pursue just any business; he wanted to identify what he was truly passionate about and go after that.

"When I was coming out of college, many kids were told by their parents what they should do," Emmet shared. "'You should be a doctor, you should be a lawyer, you should go work at a consulting firm.' I was pretty lucky in that my father didn't give me any of that guidance. He said, 'Look, you've gotta find what you're passionate about, and build a life and career around that passion.'"

With that in mind, starting a business became the subject of every conversation Emmet had—personal and professional—and the basis of every relationship he made. And it turned out that those relationships became deep and long-lasting, because everyone wanted to stay in touch with him to find out what would happen. "You almost become a walking TV show," he said. "People invest in you not from a capital perspective but from a time and energy and thought perspective." That investment would pay off in spades.

After trying to get to the bottom of what made him happy for some time, he figured it out: cars. He'd grown up playing with Matchbox cars and building model cars; by age fourteen, he wanted to buy his first car. In college, he was exposed to racing for the first time. A friend brought him to a sprint car race in Napa, and something clicked. He felt it again in 1995, when he went to his first Formula 1 race, the highest class of international racing.

The race was in Canada, and Ferrari hadn't won a race for twenty years. Meanwhile, the car's driver, a talented man by the name of John Alessi, had never won a race in his life. But the crowd had their hopes up. Alessi had all the makings of a champion; he just needed a chance to make it happen.

When he sped across the finish line in first place, it was an emotional moment. And for the first time, Emmet began to see how his personal and business purposes could align. He ended up setting what felt like a crazy goal at the time: he would start a company and take it to $1 billion in revenue. Why such an astronomical number? He knew if he achieved that goal, he'd be in a position to start a Formula 1 racing team.

When he first started talking about this billion-dollar business and the fact that he wanted to compete in Formula 1, people would look at him funny or simply start laughing. It just seemed so out there.

But little by little, he began to make headway, due in large part to his willingness to talk about what he wanted from life. In 1998, Emmet cofounded a company called iRise with the goal of dramatically accelerating software delivery by changing the way business and IT stakeholders communicate. The company invented the market for collaborative visualization and has since become the world's leading provider for software visualization, bringing him close to his billion-dollar goal.

Years after founding his company, he was at a private club in London when he struck up a conversation with a woman he'd just met—a former Olympic swimmer. He told her about his Formula 1 dream. "Well," she said, "I don't know if it matters, but I'm the personal assistant for the founder of Formula E. Would you like to meet?" Formula E is the international racing competition for electric cars.

"That definitely matters," he said. "And yes, I'd love to." Through a series of connections and events, Emmet ended up becoming a team owner in Formula 2, 3, 4, and E.

In 2007, Emmet invited Jim and his wife, Marylou, to a Formula 1 race in Long Beach, California. Having grown up in Queens, the closest Jim had ever come to such an event was a stretch of road near the beach where everyone would drag race. In Long Beach, Jim had the opportunity to witness someone else reap the benefits of the self-fulfilling prophecy.

The night before the race, Jim ended up sitting next to a young Australian fellow at dinner. The man's given name was Will Power. Will shared that if he didn't win the race the next day, he would have to quit racing. He and his parents had agreed to those terms. At the time, he was in fifth place, and Emmet explained that it would be very, very hard to win from fifth place, particularly in this race; the streets of Long Beach are narrow and winding, which makes it very challenging to pass other cars.

But the next morning, the car in first place didn't start. Neither did the car in fourth place. That meant Will was able to pass both of them right off the bat and effectively take first place by speeding past the two remaining cars. He went on to have an extraordinary career, a product of his determination that—considering his name—may or may not have been a self-fulfilling prophecy set in motion from the day he was born.

As Emmet says, "That's the magic of sharing your goals and dreams with everyone that you meet. The dots will begin to connect in unexpected ways."

LODESTAR

Ready to jump-start the self-fulfilling prophecy?

- **Envision the life you want.** The first step in bringing your dreams to fruition is getting very clear on what those dreams look like. Visualize the outcome you want, down to the very last detail.

- **Play the part.** Muhammad Ali convinced himself that he was the greatest by making it a mantra, Jim overcame his shyness by acting as a host, researchers proved that clothes and confidence can determine your future, and Rhonda Byrne instructs that believing is key to successfully manifesting. Act as if you are the person you wish to become, and eventually you will be.

- **Check your frequency.** Energy isn't just an airy-fairy concept; it has real scientific roots. The thoughts and feelings we have don't just determine our mood; they have the power to change our brain. Think about the kind of energy you're putting out into the world and what you want to achieve, and adjust accordingly.

....

CHAPTER 3

FOCUS ON THE JOURNEY, NOT THE DESTINATION: EMBRACING CHANGE AND UNCERTAINTY

In the end, we only regret the chances we didn't take, relationships we were afraid to have, and the decisions we waited too long to make.

—Lewis Carroll

WHY IS IT THAT MANY PEOPLE HESITATE TO ATTEMPT SOMETHING new, even if it sounds wildly appealing? Why is it that so many of us hold on to unsatisfying jobs—even in a favorable job market? Why do we stay in unrewarding, even abusive, interpersonal relationships? While there are no simple answers to these questions, there's one common denominator: they all require change.

That change inevitably comes with some consequential degree of uncertainty. Simply put, people do not like uncertainty. So they avoid it. And yet hiding within the unknown are the opportunities that truly make life worth living.

But what is uncertainty, really?

We can define uncertainty as a state of the unknown or the unpredictable. It seems simple, but it's one of the most vexing—and rewarding—places to be. While a few of us gravitate to the unknown, most live in fear of it—even if the certainty of our current reality is pretty bleak. As Virginia Satir, the author and psychotherapist known as "the mother of family therapy" (and, as we mentioned, a *Chicken Soup for the Soul* contributor) famously noted, "People prefer the certainty of misery to the misery of uncertainty."

Most of us understand why. Psychologically, uncertainty is highly correlated with fear and anxiety—the stress associated with the ambiguous or the unknown. The creeping sense of dread associated with uncertainty will not change the future, but it can definitely take the joy out of the present. Thus, we resist change of any kind—even if it's likely to be for the better. When it comes to behaviors, you probably won't be surprised to learn that uncertainty is frequently tied to indecision, procrastination, hesitation, and "analysis paralysis"—doing nothing for fear of doing the wrong thing. However, avoiding uncertainty often sends us on a fool's errand: we wait for the moment of absolute certainty, but that moment seldom comes. Sadly, in the wait for that perfect moment, opportunity is often lost. But it doesn't have to be that way.

If we can embrace change and the uncertainty that comes with it, we can harness more opportunities and improve the quality of our lives.

WHY IS EMBRACING CHANGE AND
UNCERTAINTY SO IMPORTANT?

To better understand uncertainty, and how to conquer it, it may be helpful to think about certainty. Certainty is a state of conviction, resoluteness, confidence, and certitude. Certainty pays off in the form of decisiveness, action, and—most importantly—an underlying sense of safety. The status quo, even if it represents stagnation, discomfort, or pain, makes us feel safe—hence Satir's observation that people prefer the certainty of misery to the misery of uncertainty.

William James, one of the founders of American psychology, noted that one's worldview—a set of assumptions about the world and our role in it—plays perhaps the most critical role in defining one's psychological health. Worldviews bring coherence and predictability to an otherwise chaotic world. They are the psychological glue of our lives. They combat uncertainty and make the world seem safe.

An example of a common worldview is that the world is just and fair. This worldview holds that, by and large, the world is a safe place and good things happen to good people. It fuels optimism and hope. But even positive worldviews can be problematic if violated. Thus, it's particularly distressing when bad things happen to good and innocent people, especially children. Another is that friends and family are inherently trustworthy. That worldview makes betrayal by the people closest to us especially devastating. Worldviews are healthiest when they are flexible, meaning there is room for "exceptions to the rule."

It's easy to see how the quest for certainty and safety via worldview formation can influence every aspect of our lives.

For example, people who ascribe to the worldview that they are worthy of happiness often strive with great tenacity to achieve it. With tenacity often comes attainment (remember our chat about the self-fulfilling prophecy?). But if a person holds the notion that they are unworthy of happiness, moments of joy are disruptive to the certainty and predictive safety of that worldview. As a result, they typically fail to strive for happiness. They are often willing to accept disappointment, as they believe it's their destiny. And when opportunities that may bring happiness roll around on their own, those people are quick to dismiss or reject them. It's just too unsafe!

Certainty and predictability are so important that human beings actually possess a biological warning system that constantly scans the environment for cues that signal conditions of uncertainty, violated expectations, and other potential threats. Buried deep within the limbic circuitry, the septo-hippocampal complex is constantly drawing comparisons to keep us safe. It's weighing our experiences against our expectations. When a "mismatch" occurs—our experiences don't match our expectations—this septo-hippocampal complex kicks into high gear. We enter into fight-or-flight mode, becoming extremely vulnerable to our surroundings. Our behavior changes too; suddenly we feel inhibited and hesitant, so much so that we're paralyzed by fear or anxiety, or even have panic attacks. But if we can "hack" our way to a sense of safety, even in uncertain conditions—if we can learn to tolerate the initial fear and vulnerability associated with uncertainty—we can harness the opportunities and healthy risks that come our way. And we can feel good doing it.

This is exactly what CVS Pharmacy CEO Helena Foulkes did back in 2014, when she took a leap into the unknown. Foulkes hated the idea that her company—whose mission it was to provide products that improved people's lives—was selling deadly cigarettes. Her own mother had died of lung cancer in 2009. She also knew that pulling the tobacco products from shelves would significantly impact CVS's bottom line and could potentially mean the end of her career.

Rather than succumb to the paralysis of indecision, Foulkes followed her gut. She removed cigarettes and other tobacco products from all 7,800 CVS retail locations and pushed antismoking products such as nicotine patches.

The fallout was financially devastating at first. CVS estimated they lost around $2 billion in annual sales with the move.[8] But by sticking to her values and weathering the storm, Foulkes was able to do something great.

Not only did CVS rebound from its initial losses, but over the course of the year, after by rebranding itself as a health-care company, it was able to reduce cigarette smoking by 1 percent in every state in which it had a presence—the equivalent of ninety-five million packs of cigarettes.[9]

By overcoming her fear of the unknown, Foulkes was able to make a huge difference in her customers' lives, all while preserving the bottom line.

Harness Your Inner Proteus

Considering its long-standing biological origins, managing uncertainty isn't a new problem—and that's good news. We can turn to history to help navigate the choppy waters of our own psyches.

You've undoubtedly heard the aphorism, "Life is a journey, not a destination." It first appeared in the 1920s in a theological context. Long before that, Ralph Waldo Emerson noted, "To finish the moment, to find the journey's end in every step of the road, to live the greatest number of good hours, is wisdom." But we can go back much, much further in time—into the depths of Greek mythology—for insight on how to navigate the journey of life most effectively. Do you remember the god Proteus? Poseidon's eldest son, Proteus, was best known for his ability to see the future and shape-shift accordingly, evading dangerous weather, disease, and death. But it wasn't just about avoiding the bad stuff. Taking on different forms allowed him to fully harness each life experience, no matter its nature.

Robert Jay Lifton's *The Protean Self: Human Resilience in an Age of Fragmentation* taps into the value of shape-shifting for mere mortals. The book was written in the early 1990s, an era marked by immense change. The result of all that change—historical dislocation, the mass-media revolution, and the threat of extinction—is what Lifton refers to as "proteanism," defined as "mutable," "versatile," and "capable of assuming many forms." Lifton believes that humans have the innate ability not only to survive the unknown but also to adapt and embrace it.

Rather than responding to constant change with fear, he writes, "We are becoming fluid and many-sided. Without quite realizing it, we have been evolving a sense of self appropriate to the restlessness and flux of our time. This mode of being differs radically from that of the past and enables us to engage in continuous exploration and personal experiment."

What's the lesson here? That flexibility in times of great change and uncertainty is key to living the life you want. But you also have to accept the truths of your current reality.

You Can Never Go Home Again—and That's a Good Thing
George was dreading his fiftieth high school reunion. He'd grown up in a little town he affectionately referred to as Leave-It-to-Beaverville. He couldn't imagine a more wholesome, wonderful place to spend one's childhood.

In fact, that was just it—he knew the experience of returning couldn't possibly live up to what he remembered. He'd driven through the town a handful of times as an adult, and it just never felt right.

"Are you looking forward to our reunion?" his high school girlfriend asked in the months leading up to the event.

"No, I'm not," he responded truthfully. He told himself maybe he shouldn't go. He'd just be disappointed, after all. Then, his daughter called and sparked a new perspective.

She was taking a class on great American writers. "Have you ever heard of Thomas Wolfe?" she asked. "We have to read his book. It's called *You Can't Go Home Again*." He hadn't read it, so he ran out to pick it up. In its pages was the solution to his reunion conundrum.

He couldn't go home again. None of us can. Our worlds are constantly changing, and that means we can never visit the same place twice—especially when many years have gone by. But that doesn't mean we can't enjoy a place in its current form. He would go and attempt to appreciate the experience for what it was *in that moment*.

When George went to the reunion, he found that the town wasn't frozen in time—not at all. Even the people who had stayed long after graduation had changed. And because he was there to enjoy everything as it was, not as it had been, he took disappointment out of the equation and had a wonderful time.

That brings us to a vital point about expectations.

Escape Expectation

So often, it's our expectations that set us up for failure. Rarely does anything turn out exactly the way we imagine it will—for better or for worse. When we surrender power to our expectations, we rob ourselves of the opportunity to experience the moment and make the best of whatever life gives us.

It can be challenging to do away with expectations altogether; we all have hopes, dreams, and fears (plus, we're too old to give our happiness over to luck, the fates, or somebody else). But if we can adjust our reactions—sparing ourselves the anguish and disappointment when things don't go our way by making lemonade out of lemons or celebrating when things go better than we imagined—we can truly enjoy the journey.

Years ago, during Jim's early years in the flower business, he partnered with an outfit in St. Louis. Jim's operation would sell roses, and the St. Louis company would fill the orders. When their contract was up, the company claimed Jim's team hadn't fulfilled their end of the bargain and that they had taken a loss as a result. So, they sued Jim's organization in federal court. At the time, he was young and very inexperienced in the ways of business—and certainly in the judicial system.

Worse, his lawyer was even younger than he was, a local kid from St. Louis. Even worse (as if that were possible), this just happened to be his first trial! The lawyer had big glasses and ears as clean as could be. Jim figured he was going to get slammed.

Would his fledgling company be able to survive this? He wrung his hands, worrying about the outcome, sweating his way through the court proceedings.

Finally, deliberation day arrived. Jim held his breath as the jury filtered into the room and delivered the verdict.

He had won the case!

Jim was astonished, but he kept his cool and calmly exited the courtroom. Afterward, he had the chance to chat with some of the jurors. They all noted how charming they found Jim's lawyer to be. The younger ones wanted to date him. The older ones thought he'd be a perfect match for their daughters. It turned out that what was said during the trial didn't matter much at all! The lawyer's bright eyes and clean ears had done all the talking. And while it didn't go the way Jim expected, it was indeed for the best—at least as far as he was concerned.

That wasn't the first time things didn't go quite as Jim had expected, with a better outcome than he had imagined.

A handful of years earlier, he had opened his first flower shop on First Avenue in New York City. At the time, he was still working full time as a social worker at St. John's Home for Boys. A friend of his managed the flower shop during the week, and he and his wife staffed it on Saturdays and Sundays, unlocking the doors in the early morning hours and shutting them only after people stopped coming in. First Avenue was also home to a host of famous restaurants—Maxwell's Plum, Proof of the Pudding. People would flock to them from the 'burbs or upstate and walk up and down the street after the meal. They'd pop into the flower shop along the way. One Saturday afternoon, a beautiful Mercedes sports coupe double-parked right in front of Jim's shop, and a gorgeous woman got out of the car. She was wearing a smart suit, complete with a perfectly tailored bolero jacket. She and Jim chatted as she looked at the merchandise on the sidewalk.

"Do you do terraces?" she asked.

"Yes, yes we do," Jim responded (he hadn't, but there was a first time for everything). She invited him over to her place, in a building called The Sovereign just a few blocks away. The Sovereign just happened to be one of the hottest apartment buildings in the city.

When Jim arrived, she introduced him to her husband, the producer and songwriter Phil Spector. The woman from the flower shop was Ronnie Spector, front woman of the Ronettes.

It was the beginning of a new service line and a wonderful friendship. And it all happened because Jim was willing to embrace an opportunity that presented itself without expectations, fake it till he made it, and see where it took him.

Trust the Process

In fact, building 1-800-Flowers into the company it's become was an exercise in embracing change and uncertainty. Jim was ten years into the flower business when he acquired a company with the 1-800-Flowers phone number and made it the name—and basis—of his whole operation. When he asked other people what they thought about his idea to make it easy to order flowers over the phone from anywhere in the country at any time of the day, some people told him how stupid they thought it was. "No one wants to call a flower shop; they want to pick out the blooms themselves. And they certainly don't need to call twenty-four hours a day," they said.

When he asked Florists' Transworld Delivery's (FTD) leadership if they were interested in partnering with him to bring his idea to life, they poo-pooed it too. Eventually, they offered him $50,000 to take it off his hands. They assured him that amount was generous; it was all but guaranteed to be a colossal failure, after all.

"Thanks, but no thanks," he responded.

While it was tough to have many tell him his plan would never work, he stuck with it, controlling what he could and tuning out the other stuff. The rest is history—and it's still being written. Today, 1-800-Flowers is exploring AI chat options that rely on voice, not text, and learn and interact nearly as well as humans do, selecting flowers your spouse would love with a series of thoughtful and intuitive questions.

Jim didn't know exactly how things would turn out, but his willingness to take the road less traveled continues to serve him in business and beyond.

Similarly, Danny Meyer followed his heart—and his gut—throughout his career, first shirking law school to pursue a career in the restaurant business. The day before he was set to take the LSAT, Danny told his uncle he wasn't really interested in becoming a lawyer. His uncle told him, "You're going to be dead a whole lot longer than you're going to be alive," and urged him to pursue what he was actually passionate about.

Danny Meyer followed his uncle's advice. He didn't apply to a single law school but instead opened his first restaurant—Union Square Cafe—at just twenty-seven.[10] Eventually, he would rewrite the rules of the fast-food chains to build Shake Shack. Shake Shack isn't your average burger joint; it's a publicly traded hamburger empire with more than four hundred locations around the world and a multibillion-dollar market cap. It started as a lowly hot dog cart in Madison Square Park, offering Chicago-style dogs and eight toppings. What set it apart—and fueled its growth—was Danny's career-long commitment to hospitality in any environment, from white-napkin establishments to paper-plate haunts.[11] That commitment to hospitality, along with a nonnegotiable side of quality, translated into Shake Shack's success. Today, he refers to

Shake Shack, which evolved to sling hamburgers, fries, milkshakes, and chicken in addition to hot dogs, as "fine casual," because the quality is no less than the food in his fine-dining establishments.

Danny Meyer is also serious about treating employees fairly, particularly in an industry where they're so often overlooked. At Shake Shack—and all of Union Square Hospitality Group's restaurants—he puts employees first.

"By putting your employees first, you have happier employees, which then leads to a higher HQ. A higher HQ leads to happier customers, which benefits all the stakeholders. The cycle is virtuous, not linear, because the stakeholders all impact each other,"[12] he said.

He remains an advocate for taking that less-traveled road in all ways, trusting his gut and doing what he feels to be the right thing—regardless of whether it seems like a profitable strategy. That approach has helped him get farther than he imagined when he first set foot in the restaurant business. As he explains, "I [think] if we somehow climb that mountain, could we potentially climb one that's a little steeper or a little bit higher—that continues to motivate me to this day."[13]

Do What Scares You

So much of what we've shared in this chapter may feel easier said than done. After all, few things are as disconcerting as uncertainty. But if you pursue only what you know, you'll go only so far. Growth is a product of vulnerability, of releasing control and seeing where the wind takes you. Only then can you take advantage of the opportunities that you didn't know were there.

Sometimes, safety is your worst enemy. We become stuck when we become afraid of fear itself. We develop a fear of flying, and then avoid it entirely, not only because we're afraid of what will happen when we go airborne but also because we've become afraid of feeling afraid. At some point, we are no longer triggered by the airplane ride itself but by the way our heart pounds when we do anything. Our stress response becomes a self-propagating spiral.

The only treatment is to break that spiral. To stick with the stuff that gets your heart pounding. The truth is, you're actually stronger and smarter when your heart is pounding—your muscles are well-nourished and ready, and your memory improves. With that in mind, engage in a little reframing. When you notice that your heart rate goes up, tell yourself you're tapping into your superpowers. As clinical psychologist, author of the book *Nervous Energy: Harness the Power of Your Anxiety*, and good friend Dr. Chloe Carmichael says, "Use the gift of anxiety." You can fear it, try to control it, or see it as an opportunity to reach the next level.

The next time you're not sure of what will happen, challenge yourself to lean into the unknown rather than avoid it. Look for the opportunities, not the potential downsides. And will yourself to embrace whatever happens, even when you're scared. As any personal trainer will tell you, you don't get stronger unless you push beyond your comfort zone—beyond your fiber tolerance. That's the only way the muscle will grow.

LESSONS FROM THE BEST SELF-HELP BOOKS ON EMBRACING CHANGE AND UNCERTAINTY

The Four Agreements by Don Miguel Ruiz

Published in 1997, *The Four Agreements* by Don Miguel Ruiz has remained on global self-help bestseller lists for over twenty-five years and has sold over twelve million copies in the United States alone. The guiding principle of Ruiz's book is that "everything we do is based on agreements we have made—agreements with ourselves, with other people, with God, and with life. But the most important agreements are the ones we make with ourselves." According to Ruiz, most suffering is self-inflicted. Thus, we have the power to transform our lives, create our own happiness, improve overall well-being, and fulfill our purposes with four life-affirming principles:

- **Be impeccable with your word.** Speaking carefully and with integrity is our primary responsibility—to ourselves and humankind (this also happens to be the hardest agreement to follow).
- **Don't take anything personally.** Knowing it isn't personal can help us avoid anger, envy, and sadness, all while boosting self-image and cultivating a happier life.
- **Don't make assumptions.** Assumptions lead to suffering, which is why they should be avoided at all costs. How do you do that? By maintaining clear communication and asking questions when any doubts arise.
- **Always do your best.** Strive to make progress toward goals by doing your best in challenges both large and small. Daily attention to this agreement helps to alleviate self-judgment and regret.

What do these agreements have to do with focusing on the journey rather than the destination? Everything, essentially. Each one encourages us to focus on the factors we can control and let go of everything else.

Who Moved My Cheese? **by Dr. Spencer Johnson**
Despite being lauded as one of the best self-help books of all time, Spencer Johnson's *Who Moved My Cheese?* isn't a self-help book at all—at least not in the traditional sense. It's an allegorical tale of four characters who live in a maze and spend their time looking for cheese. The book has sold over thirty million copies since its publication in 1998, and it remains a staple for people looking to navigate change in a healthy manner—especially in the business world.

Some of the key lessons the maze-dwellers learn over the course of the story highlight why embracing change—and the journey itself—is so important:

- **Without change, you risk extinction.** If we're too complacent—that is, simply settling for the conditions of our current environment—we stop looking for the next opportunity that will improve our lives. Nothing lasts forever, and if we don't keep our eyes peeled for possibilities, we may find ourselves stuck while the rest of the world moves on. Don't fool yourself into thinking things will stay as they are forever.

- **Don't think—MOVE.** One attribute that separates humans from other species is our ability to use logic and reason. Our brains can analyze patterns and previous experiences to predict outcomes. But that species-differentiating skill is a double-edged sword; when we fixate too much on prognostication, we can become paralyzed. Rather than wasting time and energy thinking about what achieving your goal looks like, the possibility of achieving it, or how to get there, take action. The path to our success may not be a straight line, but we won't arrive at our destination unless we move.

- **Confront fear.** When we do not have enough information to accurately forecast future events, we fill in the gaps with wild speculation that rarely has any basis in reality. We freak out about worst-case scenarios, regardless of how unlikely they are. Most often, the story we've concocted in our heads is far worse than the real challenges we'll face. Push past that fear and prosper.

The Alchemist by Paul Coelho

Similar to *Who Moved My Cheese?* Paul Coelho's 1988 novel *The Alchemist* is an allegory that contains multiple lessons for a well-lived life. It's sold over sixty-five million copies since its release, and it holds the Guinness World Record for the most-translated book by a living author. The story follows a young shepherd who, prompted by a recurring dream, sets out on a treasure-hunting mission. After navigating many trials and tribulations, he discovers the treasure he seeks is the journey itself.

Here are the lessons Santiago the shepherd learns along the way:

- **We all have a Personal Legend.** Early in the book, Santiago learns every person has what's called a Personal Legend, a concept we might better understand as our destiny or our life's purpose. If we look deep within ourselves, we might find we know what that Personal Legend is already. If we don't, we must be vigilant in looking out for it. Once we've identified our Personal Legend, it should be our life's mission to achieve it—even if that means taking some risks.

- **Fall, then get back up.** We will inevitably fail many times on the road to achieving our Personal Legend, as Santiago does. Those who continue moving forward even when they stumble are the ones who will succeed.
- **The treasure is the journey.** At the end of the novel, Santiago is told the treasure he seeks is back in Spain— under the very tree where he had the recurring dream that prompted him to action. He comes to understand that the treasure isn't a tangible one. Instead, it's the experience and insight he gained on his adventure. We are all a sum of our life's experiences, and we bring those experiences to every future choice we make. By embracing fear and change, we become that much more prepared for the next challenge.

LEAVING YOURSELF AVAILABLE FOR THE UNEXPECTED WITH SANDY CLIMAN

Media visionary Sandy Climan knows a thing or two about focusing on the journey rather than the destination. "Just a kid from the Bronx," Sandy's life has taken quite a unique path, from the northeast corner of the borough to the hallowed halls of Harvard University, and from executive roles in motion picture production to distribution, talent management, and more. Sandy has represented some of the best-known actors in the world as an agent, from Danny DeVito to Robert De Niro. He's won a BAFTA and a Golden Globe for Best Motion Picture for his work as a producer on Martin Scorsese's *The Aviator* and made history as coexecutive producer of the first digital live-action 3D film, *U2 3D*.

How did all that come about? It began with a bus ride.

Sandy's mother was a ward clerk at Bronx Municipal Hospital—part of the city hospital system in the northeast Bronx that treated more than its fair share of gunshot wounds. The hospital was affiliated with Albert Einstein College of Medicine, a private medical school. So, when Sandy got an acceptance letter from Bronx High School of Science and it specified the need to do a research project by junior year, he went someplace he'd heard of before: he took the number nine bus down Eastchester Road to Albert Einstein College of Medicine.

Sandy walked right in the door, up to the second floor, down the hall into the neurology department, and into the office of the bearded, bespectacled, pipe-smoking professor William T. Norton. Professor Norton was working to understand the myelin sheath—the layer of insulation that forms around neurons to facilitate the transmission of electrical impulses—and its role in multiple sclerosis.

"Can I stay?" Sandy asked.

Norton said yes, and for the next six years Sandy spent summers in his lab working on neurological experiments. Between that and being first in his class at one of the best high schools in the country, he had a ticket out of the Bronx—via a little school you may have heard of in Cambridge, Massachusetts.

At Harvard, Sandy majored in chemistry under the tutelage of Konrad Bloch, a Nobel Prize winner. But Sandy quickly realized he wasn't cut out for chemistry. (The good thing about being a chemistry major, however, is that no one asks you how you're doing in the subject. Once you share your major, they simply nod and move on.) He began taking classes in fine arts and secured a coveted staff position on *Harvard Lampoon*, the world's oldest continuously published humor magazine. Most importantly, he began to learn what excited him: entertainment. Instead of staying on the path everyone else wanted him to take, he got a sense of what his destiny might be.

After three years, he had enough credits to graduate, but by then he was treasurer of the *Lampoon*, and he realized he didn't want to leave. So, Sandy walked over to the School of Public Health and applied to the Master of Science in Health Policy and Management, figuring that—with less-than-stellar grades—it was a hedge against getting into business school, something he was much more interested in by then.

Ultimately, he got into both programs, and convinced the business school to count his second year in the public health program toward his MBA with just one extra course. In six years, he earned three degrees. Pretty impressive. But somehow, he was one of only three people in his graduating class at both schools to wrap up all that schooling without a job.

He'd never been west of West Virginia, where he attended National Youth Science Camp during his senior year of high school. So he cashed in his bar mitzvah bonds and bought a plane ticket to California. He figured if he could get paid to watch television and movies, that was the job for him. He hadn't really been anywhere growing up, but he knew more about the world than his well-traveled friends because he'd immersed himself in the stories he found on film. Sandy booked interviews with anyone in the business who would see him. One of those people was Rob Rothman. While he didn't hire Sandy, he made a point of staying in touch.

Sandy took the opportunities that came his way, wearing many hats and working for some of Hollywood's most legendary thinkers, strategists, and managers of talent as a result. They taught him a lot about who he wanted to be and who he didn't.

As he explains, "You learn as much what not to do from your bosses as what to do. And the trick is not to mimic them; it's to analyze them and then choose for yourself the right path." At the end of the day, the career he created was a matter of leaving expectations behind and following the twists and turns that presented.

As Sandy explains, "You leave yourself available to the unexpected." It's what he tells his kids, his colleagues, basically anyone who will listen. "Because out of that unexpected, serendipitous walk through the world, you make lifelong friends, you learn things you wouldn't learn otherwise, you correlate things that you previously thought were uncorrelated."

Ultimately, it's a winding, exciting route to a happy life.

LODESTAR

The following strategies will help you enjoy the journey and let go of the rest—expectations, fear, and more—so you can be open to all the world has in store for you.

- **Do your best and drop everything else.** We often forget that there's only so much we can control and end up spinning our wheels trying to manage factors outside of our grasp. That tendency wastes time and energy. It also keeps us from seeing opportunities that may arise in unexpected ways. Do your very best job and then let go. You'll likely be surprised by all the good that lands on your plate.

- **Keep moving.** The unknown can be paralyzing, but if you focus on putting one foot in front of the other—especially after you fall—you'll undoubtedly make progress.

- **Look for opportunities, not obstacles.** With so much working against us when it comes to embracing change, we have to hunt for reasons to open our arms. Look for all the good that may come from taking a chance, not the potential downsides.

....

CHAPTER 4

TAKE ACTION: CONQUERING TIME MANAGEMENT AND OVERCOMING PROCRASTINATION

The secret of getting ahead is getting started. The secret of getting started is breaking your complex overwhelming tasks into small manageable tasks, and then starting on the first one.

—MARK TWAIN

ARE YOU WHERE YOU WANT TO BE IN LIFE?

If the answer is no, you're not alone—as tough as it may be to admit it.

There are a lot of really, really smart people in the world. However, very few of them live up to their potential. What accounts for this frustrating reality? One of the things that gets in the way is their inability to take action or even to make a decision in the first place.

If you're at all compulsive, you probably know what we're talking about. You're likely very detail oriented—a good thing. You anticipate problems and try to solve them in advance—also good. But at some point, that attention to detail and the desire to solve even before an issue arises becomes paralyzing. So, we procrastinate. We can't move forward for fear of making a mistake. And thus we find ourselves stuck.

Like many of the other subjects we've discussed, the struggle to get a handle on time management and procrastination isn't new—though it isn't quite as old as some other conundrums. The dawn of the Industrial Revolution launched the need for a new relationship between people and time. While agricultural work allowed for wiggle room (one could rise more or less with the sun without too much hassle from the animals and quit when the work was done for the day), factories required that people operate by the clock. The mantra became, to borrow from Benjamin Franklin in *The Way to Wealth*, "Waste neither time nor money, but make the best use of both."

In 1911, Frederick Winslow Taylor, an American mechanical engineer, published his time-management methodologies in a book, *The Principles of Scientific Management*, with the goal of increasing worker productivity. With so much to make and do, the art and science of time management took off, embraced by those running factory lines and occupying corner offices. While a lot has changed since the early 1900s, the need for effective time management has only grown. From Marie Curie to Peter Drucker and James Clear, great thinkers and teachers have taken on the gargantuan task of using their time as effectively as possible. In this day and age, it's not all about work—there's also so much out there to enjoy. As Franklin said in *Poor Richard's Almanack*, "Dost thou love life? Then do not squander time, for that is the stuff life is made of." It turns out, however, that life today is also made up of a whole lot of distractions.

Why Is Time Management So Important?

It's crucial to point out that managing your time is not just about getting things done and checking tasks off a list. In fact, if you get too caught up in the hustle of it all, you might find yourself looking up and realizing your life has passed you by.

Jim's friend Dave Kerpen, author of the *New York Times* bestseller *Likeable Social Media: How to Delight Your Customers, Create an Irresistible Brand, and Be Generally Amazing on Facebook (And Other Social Networks)*, warns against falling prey to hustle culture. Dave says that "the grind" is often romanticized as a key to success, but it can take a real toll on the quality of our lives. He cites a 2019 study of dying people's regrets, which found that most people wished they had spent less time working and more time with loved ones. As Dave explains, "Not once did someone say, 'I wish I had worked harder.'" With that in mind, Dave says that "perhaps it's time to break away from the hustle culture and start setting our priorities. We all have different things that are important to us, whether it's spending time with family, taking care of our health, or simply getting enough rest." It's time we honored them.

To make sure we're fulfilling our individual priorities, Dave recommends setting your own BAIT: Boundaries Around

Important Times. Those boundaries ensure the most important aspects of your life get your valuable attention. For Dave, that looks like putting work aside for the day at three o'clock to pick up his son from school and maintaining a calendar that allows him to schedule meetings while protecting a handful of precious hours to focus on work tasks.

"By prioritizing what's important to you," Dave says, "you can avoid the regrets that may come with the hustling lifestyle. You can achieve success without sacrificing your health, relationships, or well-being."

We all know the phrase "time is money," but the truth is, time is far more valuable than money because it is a finite resource. We have only so much of it. You can always amass more wealth, but no matter what you do, there are only twenty-four hours in a day. As such, understanding what's most important to you is the first step in managing your time to align with your values and your goals—and to building a regret-free life.

"We Later Found Out" Doesn't Count

Technology distracts the average working person every forty seconds. If that weren't bad enough, according to a study from the University of California, Irvine, it takes about twenty-three minutes and fifteen seconds to get back to the task at hand once you've been distracted. That means it's absolutely critical to take back your time if you want to get anything done—let alone achieve your biggest goals. Sometimes, those distractions come in the form of information. With so much to learn, it can feel as if there's always more to analyze before choosing a particular path. Paralysis and procrastination sneak in, and we find ourselves stuck.

But most of the time, it's best to bite the bullet and move forward with the information you have.

In therapy, George has worked with numerous people in life-and-death professions—doctors, first responders, and crisis managers of all kinds. Just as with any job, mistakes are made sometimes and—sadly—people die prematurely. A surgeon might come to him, telling him she inadvertently destroyed someone else's life and so she's destroying her own in various ways. A firefighter may tell him he can't sleep because he's wracked by guilt about a botched rescue. The weight of what's happened is real, of course, but it's getting in the way of not only their productivity but also their health and happiness.

One of the questions he asks is, "When you made the decision, were you reasonably sure the outcome would be positive?" Most people say yes.

What he says next typically shocks them: "Then you made the right decision."

"Well, we later found out ... " they tend to say, offering up insights about where things went wrong.

"Stop," George replies. "It doesn't count. If you moved forward based on what you knew, you did the right thing."

We typically judge decisions by one of two criteria: process and outcome. Ninety-nine percent of the time, it's the latter. We think of the world in terms of wins or losses. What we need to do instead is judge our decisions by process. That's quite hard to do because we're an outcome-based society. We congratulate people not on how they handled a tough situation but on what they ultimately accomplished.

Instead, work on judging your decision retrospectively by the process, not the outcome. That way, when a challenging issue arises, you'll understand that you're equipped to handle it—and that you know *how* it's done. You can use those insights to avoid paralysis and procrastination. With that in mind, it's important to think about how we manage our time.

What's Your Propensity?

Are you a squirrel or a sloth when it comes to your to-do list?

Do you find yourself working on one thing, only to shift gears as soon as something else enters your field of awareness? While that polyphasic tendency can work in your favor from time to time, it can also be remarkably paralyzing—when we do ten things at once, it's hard to accomplish anything at all.

On the flip side, focusing exclusively—and painstakingly— on one task to the detriment of any and all things around you feeds procrastination as well. It's easy to tell yourself you'll start on the next thing as soon as you finish this one, only to find your-self wrapped up in a single issue for days, weeks, or even years at a time. Regardless of your tendency, it's up to you to make it a strength and not a liability.

The way out of the time and attention warp begins with knowing your propensity. What do you tend to do, and how does it get in the way of what you *need* to do?

If you're a squirrel, likely to get distracted throughout the day by this, that, or the other thing, put the items that have to get done ASAP at the top of your list. Get to them first, before the other stuff gets in the way. This is particularly helpful if a to-do requires that you set it into motion and let it take its course. George calls it the incubator effect. For example, if you need an insurance quote, you have to first call the insurance company, but it may take time for them to get back to you with a number. If you're having a medical issue, it may take a while to get in to see the doctor and get the help you need. The first step, however, is making the appointment. Or maybe you just need to get something into the slow cooker with at least a handful of hours to spare so you can have it cooked in time for dinner. If it has an incubation period of some sort, start that project now and let the process unfold.

Be Discerning about What You Do
Managing your time and your progress is as much about *what* you choose to do as it is about *how* you choose to do it. Jim's first job was as a live-in night counselor at St. John's Home for Boys in Queens, New York. His workday would start around four o'clock in the afternoon and wrap up at midnight. That meant his shift overlapped with the day's staff, including a woman they referred to as the "house mother" (it was the '70s, what can we say?). She would cook for the residents and staff alike, and every night, they'd sit down to dinner together before she left. Then, it would just be Jim and his ten guys until he was "off duty." But because the crew was so skeletal, he was the only staff member there all night long— and thus responsible for responding to any issues overnight and getting the boys out the door for school in the morning.

After proving he could handle things on his own, he was given a job running a group home like the one where he'd cut his teeth, this time all on his own. Shortly thereafter, a boy was transferred there from a facility in Staten Island that had burned down. The boy, whom we'll call Jake, was kind, intelligent, handsome, and perhaps—as Jim came to believe—the reason for the fire.

The home in Queens was quite close to the Van Wyck Expressway. One night, Jake went to a party on the other side of the expressway. To get back, he could either walk two long blocks to Liberty Avenue and cross at the viaduct or travel three long blocks in the opposite direction and cross at 109th Avenue. Jake chose neither. Instead, he walked right across the expressway—a shortcut that ultimately cut his life short. He was hit by a car and killed.

Jim was twenty-two at the time. He didn't really report to anyone, so he had to figure out what to do alone. He contacted the members of Jake's family he could find, made arrangements, and held a wake and a funeral. After shaking hands with the last guest, he realized something. Everything he'd done to date in that role and the one before had been reactive. If a kid got in trouble at school, he'd go handle it. If someone was acting out, he'd step in. And now, in the face of tragedy, he'd found himself scrambling. That needed to change.

Over the course of several months, he visited group homes like his and spoke to people doing similar work. He noticed that those who were good at their jobs came to work with a plan. They set up schedules, ran activities, and followed a codified protocol when incidents occurred. Jim decided that, to be successful in this role—or any role, really—he had to get it together when it came to time management.

Soon after, he was promoted into an administrative role, working for the man who ran the whole agency—a true time-management freak. Under his tutelage, Jim learned how to budget his time, make lists, prioritize tasks.

Those skills came in quite handy when he opened his first flower shop and once again found himself wearing every hat in the place. Eventually, he prided himself on being the best floral designer, salesperson, delivery guy, and more. In fact, he was very good at those things—thanks to his time-management training, he'd found a way to succeed at them all. Plus, he was willing to work longer and harder and more efficiently than everyone else. On Thanksgiving, he would take the off-route deliveries, putting the arrangements in the back of the car with the kids on the way to his parents' house for dinner. He knew taking on those extra orders would make the delivery truck more efficient. At the end of the day, it was handling those tedious tasks that helped him—and his burgeoning business—thrive.

But, of course, as Marshall Goldsmith wisely wrote, what got you here won't get you there. Jim learned the slow, hard lesson that it was often better to focus on the things only he could do and hire others to handle the rest—even if they couldn't do it quite as well as he could.

One day, a couple of decades later, he'd be reminded of the importance of delegation once again. At the time, he was operating a dozen flower shops, and his father-in-law—an engineer—came to visit. The refrigerator had just broken, and Jim picked up the phone to call a repairman.

"Wait a minute," his father-in-law said. He took the whole damn thing apart, looked at the schematics, fixed the issue, and put it back together—wondering aloud from time to time why Jim would call someone when they could figure it out themselves.

That evening, Jim was feeling down about the whole thing. He didn't have his father-in-law's knowledge or skills or propensity for mechanics. But then a light bulb went on. There were things he could do that neither his father-in-law nor a repairman could. And frankly, he could make a lot more money doing them well in the same period of time it would take a repairman to fix the fridge. Further, if he were to take on the repairs himself, it would probably have taken him ten times the amount of time to make it work—if he could do it at all. It was yet another lesson in time management: Figure out what you can and can't do well and do the things you're best at. Fire yourself from the rest.

Time management has been a lifelong journey for him ever since—a continuing evolution influenced in part by the people he's encountered along the way.

LESSONS FROM THE BEST SELF-HELP BOOKS ON TIME MANAGEMENT

***How to Get Control of Your Time and Your Life* by Alan Lakein**
Time-management expert and author Alan Lakein presented a solution to navigating the hustle of work and beyond with his book *How to Get Control of Your Time and Your Life*, which was first published in 1973 and has sold over three million copies to date.

In his book, Lakein describes a matrix that can be used to determine how best to proceed when we're paralyzed by what to do next. As he explains, there are things that are both urgent and important, and thus should be tackled right away. There are things that are neither urgent nor important; those can be put off indefinitely. The trap lies with the things that are urgent but not important, or important but not urgent. In the messy middle of the matrix, we get stuck. We struggle to differentiate between urgency and importance. So, we waste our time doing things that seem urgent but really aren't that important, or the stuff that is important but really could be postponed. (If you've ever found yourself slipping down the rabbit hole of answering emails when you've got a much more pressing deadline, you know exactly what he's talking about.)

The solution is ultimately answering what was appropriately named *Lakein's Question*: "What is the best use of my time right now?" To do that, you have to be willing to move forward with the information you have at this very moment. As Lakein wrote, "Time = Life. Therefore, waste your time and waste your life, or master your time and master your life."

Rich Dad, Poor Dad by Robert Kiyosaki and Sharon Lechter

Rich Dad, Poor Dad is somewhat of an outlier in the best self-help books of all time because its primary message centers on financial literacy. Released in 1997 by Robert Kiyosaki and Sharon Lechter, it outlines important and practical principles about building wealth through illustrative parables from Kiyosaki's childhood.

Kiyosaki and Lechter share that one of the primary reasons middle-class earners never break through the wealth ceiling is because they have a flawed understanding of *how* to accumulate wealth. In the chapter "The Rich Don't Work for Money," the "poor dad" works endlessly in pursuit of money, while the "rich dad" character leverages a more valuable asset—time.

Here are the ways Kiyosaki and Lechter believe effective time management leads to wealth:

- **Time is money.** It's an age-old saying, but how many of us actually know what our time is worth? The poor and middle class rarely assign enough value to the hours in their day, resulting in a vast waste of resources. The rich, on the other hand, have the ability to see what their time is worth (remember Jim's encounter with a broken fridge?). The rich know the opportunity cost of their time. If the net gain of delegation is higher, they'll choose that option every time.

- **Stability is a trap.** The poor and middle class are on a quest for security and stability. As a result, they end up staying too long in dead-end jobs that are heavy on stability but light on mobility. The comfort is paralyzing, and it quickly trumps their desire for wealth. It also blinds them to the opportunities that present themselves to break out of their unhealthy cycles. The rich recognize these opportunities and seize them because they are not afraid of leaving their comfort zones in search of something better.

Atomic Habits by James Clear

When compared to the other titles in this book, James Clear's *Atomic Habits* is the new kid on the block—but that doesn't mean the content is any less valuable. Published in 2018, *Atomic Habits* has quickly become a staple on self-help shelves, selling nearly five million copies to date.

Clear says the secret to managing time is all about having the right habits. Adopting the right habits—and ditching the bad ones—will make you more productive and drastically improve your life. But to do so, you must understand how habits work and how you can change yours. He argues that most people fail to achieve their goals and get bogged down by procrastination not because they lack motivation or the proper skills but because their systems doom them from the start. Here's what you should do instead:

- **Attach habits to your identity.** The way you spend your time each day is a result of who you believe yourself to be, consciously or unconsciously. Decide on an identity—an artist, an effective employee, maybe a time-management expert—and ask yourself: *How would a person with that identity spend their time?* Then do those things. Eventually, your actions will dictate your new identity.

- **Get intentional.** We think that freedom is good and structure is bad, but we're actually wired to crave structure. When we have too many choices, we'll always pick the easy one—which results in procrastination. Get intentional by making clear statements about the things you want to accomplish. "I will [BEHAVIOR] at [TIME] in [LOCATION]." Those clear statements will better structure your habits and your day.

- **Bundle your habits.** Pair actions you *want* to do with actions you *need* to do, like listening to your favorite podcast *only* when you're exercising. The reward makes the needed action more attractive, which means you're more likely to accomplish it.

- **Increase friction.** Curbing procrastination and maximizing your time is all about making the unproductive bad habits harder to do. Add as many steps as possible between you and the bad habit, and you'll be less likely to do it. This might look like unplugging your TV or putting your phone in another room. The more time and effort it takes to perform the bad habit, the less likely you are to be tempted by it.

A LESSON FROM BOB LESSIN

One of the most productive and efficient people Jim has ever met was named Bob Lessin. Bob was a Wall Street legend, and working his magic with the markets meant he was on a tight timeline. He'd invite you to meet him for breakfast at a local restaurant, for instance, and as soon as you arrived, your meal did too. He'd talk through the issue at hand as you made quick work of your poached eggs and toast, then thank you for coming as an assistant swooped in to pick up your plate—all in twenty minutes flat. When you got up, he'd stay put. There was a queue of people waiting to take your place. And before you could make it to the door, the table would be cleaned and restocked, with a new guest seated in front of Bob.

One of the most valuable lessons he imparted was on the value of an agenda. It ensured he and his team got in and out of meetings with all their bases covered and checklists taken care of. He was truly the master of the twenty-minute meeting, with or without breakfast.

Any time you were on the phone with him, he also had one of his assistants on the line, quietly taking notes and ensuring all to-dos and follow-up items were taken care of. And somehow, he made time to play two hours of tennis with an instructor every day—even after a stroke threatened to strip him of his ability to walk at just forty-one years old.

He was deliberate about how he spent his time and his money. He had beautiful homes all over the world, but whenever he flew, he flew coach. He just thought anything else was a complete waste. So there he'd be, jetting across the world in the last row, middle seat. He'd emerge from the aircraft slightly disheveled, with a fanny pack in tow. But rather than invoking condescending looks from his peers, they found themselves wondering if they should be more like him and save the extra cash they spent on first-class tickets. Unfortunately, Bob passed at a very young age from leukemia. But his legacy as a highly effective and efficient leader—and a wonderful friend—lives on.

LODESTAR

The best time to take control of your schedule and quit procrastinating? You guessed it: right now. How do you get the ball rolling?

- **Bait yourself to stay true to your priorities.** It's easy to get caught up in hustle culture and the idea that doing more is the only way to achieve our goals. But the reality is, the true measure of our success is whether or not we are staying true to our own priorities. With that in mind, we must understand what we want in life before we can effectively manage our time.

- **Make a decision with the information you have.** Sure, having more insight into a particular situation can be helpful. But don't let the search for additional data keep you from making progress. The best decision you can make is the one you can arrive at with the information at hand.

- **Be discerning about the tasks you take on.** There's a time and a place to tackle everything there is to do—like when you're starting a new business with very few resources. But most of the time, your goals will be better served by taking on the roles you're best at and outsourcing the rest.

- **Work on your habits.** We are ultimately the way we spend our time. Be intentional about what you do on a daily basis by optimizing your habits and weeding out the ones that don't serve you.

....

CHAPTER 5

DON'T WORRY, BE HAPPY: LETTING GO OF DEPRESSION, SHAME, AND GUILT

When you know better, you do better.

—MAYA ANGELOU

SOMETIMES OUR VERY HUMAN EMOTIONS CAN FEEL LIKE DIRTY words. If you've ever felt shame—and, as a human being, it's pretty much inescapable—you probably know what we mean.

In today's world, shame is challenged in self-help, psychology, and beyond. It's the monster lurking in the shadows of our psyches. But you can avoid its grip—and even use it as a catalyst for progress—if you know how to let go. To do that, you've got to understand the complex relationship between shame and its lesser evils: guilt and regret.

First, let's clarify how we are using these three words. The ample supply of books, talks, and articles on shame has muddled the message a bit, seemingly accepting Humpty Dumpty's perspective in Lewis Carroll's *Through the Looking-Glass*: "When I use a word," Humpty Dumpty says to Alice, "it means just what I choose it to mean—neither more nor less." (This is why George remains a dedicated fan of the *Oxford English Dictionary*.) Here are our three words and how we're defining them, with the help of the OED:

- **Guilt:** "The fact of having committed a specified or implied offense or crime." We're talking about culpability here.
- **Regret:** "A feeling of sadness, repentance, or disappointment over something that has happened or been done." In other words: sorrow, remorse, contrition.
- **Shame:** "A painful feeling of humiliation or distress caused by the consciousness of wrong or foolish behavior." Humiliation is the name of the game.

When you look at the relationship between the three words, you'll notice a cascading, intensifying effect. It begins with guilt or perceived culpability (we believe we're to blame for a particular activity), moves into regret (we feel bad about it), and culminates in a deeply felt sense of shame, or humiliation. The trick is to learn how to stop the cascade before you drown in the deluge. Or, if you are already at the bottom of the waterfall, how to swim out. Understanding how the three interact can set you free.

WHY IS LETTING GO OF GUILT, REGRET, AND SHAME SO IMPORTANT?

In the tumble of guilt, regret, and shame, most people would agree that shame is the most intense. It's definitely one of the least desirable on the list of human emotions; nobody wants to feel ashamed. Guilt comes down to who's to blame (if you're feeling guilt, it may be you, unfortunately). Regret can be a natural and healthy response to that guilt. Shame takes it a step further, to a darker and less productive place (humiliation is no joke, and it can be hard to escape).

If we can intervene before shame steps in, we can break free before the going gets too tough—and even use those emotions to our advantage.

Imagine you're fighting somebody who's a lot bigger and stronger than you are—that scary shame monster. If you decide to exchange head blows, you're probably going to lose. But if you realize your three-hundred-pound opponent is supported by two relatively weak knees, and you attack one of them, an interesting thing happens. All of a sudden, the monster drops down to your level. And if you've done enough damage to that weak spot, they can't navigate very well. If you change tactics, you might actually survive.

Understand Culpability

For many of us, feeling in control is important. Meanwhile, feeling out of control is anxiety-provoking—terrifying, even. So, we may find ourselves taking responsibility for things, even negative things, over which we had no real control. But the greatest form of control is actually knowing what you can and cannot control. With that in mind, let's go back to culpability. There are four perspectives on culpability. Two can be helpful, two, not so much. When things go badly:

- You can accept responsibility for things over which you have no real control. This is a fool's errand. It is endless and exhausting.

- You can deny responsibility for things over which you really did have control. This dysfunctional coping mechanism was proliferated by baby boomer parents trying to protect the assumed fragile egos of their millennial children. And of course, those millennials are teaching it to their children. Unfortunately, this tactic gives rise to a victim mentality and a culture of fragility. It is also self-destructive, because only through accepting responsibility for your failures can you begin to overcome them.

- You can accept partial responsibility, as appropriate. Frankly, life is a team sport. Successes and failures are shared. We're all better off when we acknowledge that reality and take responsibility for that which is ours and move on. Diffusing responsibility in this way can also lessen the burden of mistakes and failures and help you move forward faster.

- You can accept responsibility in the rare instances when you are indeed solely responsible for mistakes and failure. When you do, you instantly distinguish yourself from the majority of people who deny their responsibility, even when it's due. By accepting due responsibility, you come to understand how to correct the problem (when possible), but more importantly, you come to understand how to prevent it from happening in the future.

As you consider your culpability in any given situation, it's important to remember the great Maya Angelou's wise words: "When you know better, you do better." And you will do better in the future. The road to some of the greatest successes in your life will be paved with failure. Realizing that—and accepting it—is key to getting where you want to go. If you did the best you could with the knowledge you had, you've got to let it go and move on. It's time to focus on the future.

CHOOSE A DIFFERENT NARRATIVE

Sometimes, switching up that narrative can make all the difference.

Take Jim's college experience. It wasn't exactly something to write home about—especially his first attempt at higher education. He had attended an all-boys Catholic high school in Brooklyn and loved it. He thrived in that environment, with lots of close friends and ample confidence.

Then he and his buddy decided to leave New York City for a small commuter college on the Jersey Shore. It wasn't far from the Queens neighborhood where he grew up, but for all intents and purposes, it was a world away. Jim's buddy had a big personality; he adjusted pretty well to college life, and he went home every weekend to see his friends and family. Jim, on the other hand, couldn't afford to make the trek back and forth so frequently. He went from feeling very secure in high school to being a shy kid far from home, trying to develop a new group of friends in a place where most people didn't stick around to hang out.

He didn't adjust socially and didn't do well in his classes as a result. After two years, his performance was so abysmal that he left before the administration could kick him out.

Slowly, he got himself together, working and going to school part time at John Jay College of Criminal Justice.

You know what happened next: He bought a retail flower shop, and a handful of years after that, the company acquired the 1-800-Flowers phone number and disrupted the floral industry. The rest is history.

Today Jim sits on the board of John Jay. At a recent strategic planning meeting, the top brass began talking about the need to get the school's four-year graduation rate up.

"Why?" Jim asked.

"Well, it helps with our rankings," was the reply.

"I gotta tell you," Jim responded, "my seven years here were some of the best seven years of my life."

The room got quiet. Mouths gaped. But he was sharing a crucial lesson about reframing. Over the years, Jim has (with humor) embraced what many might see as something to be ashamed of and made it a vital part of his legend.

We should all be thinking about what our narrative could be, should be, and will be. How do we make our difficult moments into moments we're proud of? When we transform the narrative, we dam up the flood of guilt, regret, and shame. We transform the most painful moments of our lives into stories we have power over rather than experiences that have power over us.

With that said, it's important to note that there can be power in pain too.

Channel Pain into Power

At a conference Jim attended, a woman got up on stage and bravely shared the story of her fourteen-year-old son, whom she had lost to suicide. He had been bullied online without the family's knowledge. Instead of drowning in guilt, regret, and shame, the woman channeled her pain into purpose. She went after the social media companies that enabled and exacerbated anonymous bullying. She was not a failure of a parent plagued by guilt, dragging around the burden of responsibility for her son's death. She was a parent who took up the torch, fighting to save countless young people from suffering a similar fate. And she succeeded, shutting down some of the platforms on which her son was bullied so other kids and families wouldn't experience the same pain.

Jim has met other parents who have challenged and changed laws regarding opioid prescriptions after their children died from overdoses. He has collaborated with others who have organized to stop the vaping crisis after their kids fell prey to predatory marketing tactics. It's evidence that we can let pain destroy us or we can make the choice to channel that pain into productivity. When we choose the latter, our loss not only helps others—it transforms us as well.

Pain is just energy. You are the conduit. And that means you get to choose what to do with it.

Own Your Story—Even When It's Ugly
Occasionally, successfully navigating guilt, regret, and shame is a matter of owning up to your missteps and mistakes—big and small. Jim's friend Kevin O'Neill has built a very successful executive search firm called Acertitude. Upon meeting him, a polished professional with a confident smile, you might think he's always had it all together. But around Christmas every year, he sends out a letter telling a very different story.

Years ago, Kevin was managing the responsibilities of work and a young family. On Christmas Eve, he left the house with $300 in his pocket to buy gifts for his children and wound up at a local bar instead.

Later that night, he found himself lying in the street, that $300 gone, with nothing to show for it. It was an incredibly low moment—perhaps the lowest of his life.

Recently, Jim called him to ask why he continues to send out that letter. That moment has faded into the rearview, after all.

"Well," Kevin replied, "it's a confession of sorts. It reminds me of where I was. And I hope it serves as inspiration for others who might be in a similar spot, suffering the way I was. I hope they'll read it and see that there's a way out."

It's a story that could evoke a lot of shame. Instead, Kevin owns it. All that energy that would be channeled into shame is now available for other pursuits. Plus, because he's using what he's been through to help others, he's attracting more positive energy and ultimately more success.

When you own your most shameful secret, you set yourself free. You turn that shame into power—power to do more and to enable others to find a life outside of their shame too. That's a beautiful thing. Plus, you never know how the most difficult events will transpire. So often, they make us who we are.

Be Too Ashamed to Fail

Jim's first dozen years in the flower business were marked by failure. There were countless times when he could've given up, but he didn't. He was just too ashamed to pull the plug. He knew that if he did, that failure would be made official. So he just kept going.

Finally, in his early thirties, he found himself on solid footing. And then things went downhill. A flower company called 1-800-Flowers launched in Dallas, Texas. Jim thought it was the best idea he'd ever heard. So he called them and asked to become the fulfilling florist for their orders in the New York City area. Things were going swimmingly—the company had become quite important to his business—until the orders suddenly stopped.

Jim called the leadership team in Dallas to see what was going on.

"Business isn't going well," he was told. "Pretty much everyone here has been laid off."

So, he got on an American Airlines flight to Dallas and offered to buy the company. They took him up on his offer.

But back then, he still didn't know much about bankers and lawyers and accountants and this thing called due diligence. Instead, he had not done any due negligence. He bought the company without knowing what its balance sheet looked like. He figured he was saving money by leaving the lawyers and accountants out of it.

What he had actually done was personally sign for all of the company's debts. He'd put $2 million into the business and owed another $7 million. That was the bad news.

It *was* humiliating. Over the previous ten years, he had worked seven days a week to operate twenty flower shops in total. Things were looking up. Now he was broke again.

The good news was that his grandmother told him bankruptcy was not an option for him. He had no choice but to dig himself out of that hole. He had no choice but to think big, have good luck, and build a national company. That meant there was no time to do little things. He had to make big moves.

The five-year climb out of that hole was vicious—more grueling than the previous ten years. Along the way, he realized that little old Jim could do something beneficial for the bigwigs, people who had the assets he needed to succeed. He found friends in powerful people such as Ted Turner, who gave him the opportunity to advertise on CNN, and the company eventually became *the* national brand in its category.

In the end, the worst deal of his life turned out to be the best one. What made all the difference? He was too ashamed to fail.

As you can see, shame isn't all bad. It can be a serious motivator to do and be more. With that in mind, if you don't know better, if you can't do better *yet*, just keep moving.

When Depression Sneaks In

The weight of guilt, regret, and shame often sheds light on another heavy state: depression. (We must note here that we're talking about *situational* depression and not the clinical diagnosis.) People believe their terrible circumstances—and the guilt, regret, and shame that come with them—cause depression. But they don't.

Let's say a single mom loses her job and feels stressed. She's not sure how she'll pay the mortgage, and now she feels as if she can't get out of bed in the morning. She thinks she wouldn't be depressed if she hadn't lost her job. Virtually every country song out there has a similar take: "I lost my girlfriend, my pickup truck, my good ol' dog. If they come back to me, I'll be happy again." But they confuse correlation with causality. It's not loss that causes depression—it's what we tell ourselves *about* the loss. As Epictetus said, "Men are not disturbed by things, but by the views which they take of things." In other words: It's not what happens to you that matters. It's how you interpret it. Cognitive scientists have been telling us this for years.

It's not that the woman who lost her job doesn't have a legitimate reason to be stressed. How is she going to pay the mortgage?

Who's going to put food on the table for the kids? Those are very real concerns. But if that's where it ends, that's where *she* ends. Alternatively, she can choose to let the shame mobilize her. If shame motivates you to *take action*, then it's not so bad.

Once again it comes back to narrative and to the famous words of Henry Ford: "Whether you think you can, or you think you can't—you're right."

A key to stopping the cascade of guilt, regret, and shame is to view failure as a stepping stone instead of a self-fulfilling prophecy. When failure feels like an inevitable end, we quit. But when it feels like a stepping stone, the only rational thing to do is keep going.

All those failures, mistakes, and regretful moments in your life? Embrace them. Shout them from the rooftops. Make them a proud part of your story. They're how you will arrive at what comes next.

LESSONS FROM THE BEST SELF-HELP BOOKS ON GUILT, REGRET, AND SHAME

You Can Heal Your Life by Louise Hay

Released in 1984, Louise Hay's *You Can Heal Your Life* is one of the bestselling self-help books of all time, with over fifty million copies sold since its release. Hay's central theory is that illnesses of the body are rooted in the mind and that disorders can be healed through the powers of positive thinking and mental well-being.

Hay shares with readers that the answer to internal strife is within each of us. In fact, life is very simple: what we give out, we get back. When we feed our sadness or anxiety with more of the same, we give away our power, and "what we believe about ourselves and about life becomes true for us"—sounds like a self-fulfilling prophecy, doesn't it?

A key tenet of overcoming mental maladies is to realize that the power is in the present moment. In a world that tells us to seek external validation and remedies, we often forget that we have the innate ability to achieve happiness and self-fulfillment on our own terms. Hay encourages readers daily to take stock of what they feel with two simple questions: Is it negative or positive? Do you want this thought to be creating your future? If not, it's time to cast it away.

As Hay shares, "When we create peace and harmony and balance in our minds, we will find it in our lives."

Don't Sweat the Small Stuff . . . and It's All Small Stuff by Richard Carlson

Before he became a bestselling author, Richard Carlson was a psycho-therapist who worked specifically with people experiencing great stress. He took concepts that you might find in the spirituality section of a bookstore—gratitude, meditation, loving-kindness, awareness of mortality—and offered them to his readers as practical tools to reduce their angst and create more peace and joy in their lives.

It was wisdom people sorely needed. When the book came out in 1997, it shot right to the *New York Times* bestseller list, where it comfortably sat for 101 weeks. Carlson's two-pronged thesis is right there in the title: (1) Don't sweat the small stuff, and (2) it's all small stuff. Offering gentle insight, he encourages readers to view life through the lens of what matters most. From that perspective, problems tend not to loom quite so large. Even the cascade of guilt, regret, and shame can be shifted when you take a mindful step back.

Don't Sweat the Small Stuff is a beautiful road map for how to bring more peace and happiness into your life. Here are a few of our favorite gems:

- **Adopt a different perspective.** Sometimes a simple point-of-view shift can do wonders. It can pave the way for peace and relaxation—and it has a way of making things far easier to manage. An eighteen-wheeler in the fast lane may seem unpassable when you're on the highway in a Volkswagen Beetle. But when you're in an airplane, that truck seems no bigger than an actual beetle.
- **Don't forget to be human.** Carlson does a beautiful job reminding us to lean into patience, compassion, generosity, gratitude, and kindness—the human emotions that can be hard to access when we're caught up in shame. This not only helps us improve the way we feel about ourselves but also uplifts the people around us too.
- **Take small steps.** Change doesn't have to be radical. You can practice small actions and new ways of thinking every day. Long before we learned to run, we learned to walk. And how did we do that? By taking baby steps.

Daring Greatly: How the Courage to Be Vulnerable Transforms the Way We Live, Love, Parent, and Lead by Brené Brown

Before she took to the international stage, Brown was a social worker, researcher, and professor who spent more than two decades of her life studying courage, vulnerability, and shame. Her gift is in her ability to unpack complex topics and make them universally accessible. Since then, she has successfully parlayed her academic work into a popular message that educates and enlightens.

When Brené Brown burst onto the scene in 2004 with her first book, *Women and Shame*, people started paying attention. By the time *The Gifts of Imperfection* came out in 2010, she was well on her way to becoming a household name. And when *Daring Greatly* was published two years later, Brené officially took the world by storm. As of this writing, she's written six #1 *NYT* bestsellers, given five TED Talks, hosted two immensely popular podcasts, and even has her own feature documentary on Netflix. You've probably seen her viral TED Talk on the power of vulnerability—and if you haven't, stop reading and go watch it.

Brown believes vulnerability is at the core of all human feelings—not just guilt and shame, but positive feelings such as love, joy, and passion. She makes a strong case for courageously embracing more vulnerability in our lives.

For one, vulnerability makes you strong, not weak. Brown challenges the long-held assumption that strength means being tough and hardening ourselves against the world. She argues that leaning into the things that make us feel most vulnerable is itself a dazzling act of courage.

When it comes to shame, Brown argues that verbalizing it helps you understand it—and let it go. Learning to speak your shame out loud builds resilience. It also lightens the weight on your shoulders, stripping shame of its power to suffocate your joy.

BOUNCING FORWARD WITH RICK PITINO

In March 2000, right after Toronto Raptors superstar Vince Carter sunk a three-pointer to beat the Boston Celtics at the buzzer, Celtics head coach Rick Pitino lost his cool. It was his third season coaching the Celtics and the team's thirty-fourth loss that season.

He had been brought in to bring back Boston basketball, but the team was struggling under his leadership.

"Larry Bird is not walking through that door, fans," Pitino said. "Kevin McHale is not walking through that door and Robert Parish is not walking through that door. And if you expect them to walk through that door, they're going to be gray and old. . . . All this negativity that's in this town sucks. . . . It stinks. It makes the greatest city in the world lousy."[14]

Pitino's frustration stemmed from the negativity coming out of the Boston media during the 1999–2000 NBA season. Pundits accused Pitino, who'd led the University of Kentucky to an NCAA championship three years prior, of having lost his magic touch. The criticism became too much for him; he quit halfway through the next season. On the heels of three straight losing seasons, the once mighty coach ended his Celtics tenure with a 102–146 record. Worse, he became a metaphor for failure, his prestigious reputation stained.

But rather than wallow, Pitino chose to try again with a different team. He believed that success was a choice, and he applied that maxim with a new squad at the University of Louisville. He knew he'd disgraced his career by failing in front of the ravenous Boston fans, but he didn't let it become an excuse to stop. He even acknowledged his postgame meltdown by parodying it to the Louisville press during the 2005 season.

He was committed to finishing out his career on his own terms and establishing a legacy he could be proud of. The perseverance paid off. In 2013, Pitino's Louisville Cardinals won the NCAA tournament, and he became the first NCAA Division I coach in history to win a title at two different schools.

Yes, Pitino has his place in the Boston Celtics Hall of Shame. But by letting go of the past and looking for a new opportunity to succeed, he also secured his place in the Naismith Memorial Basketball Hall of Fame. And it's proof that you have control over when you call it quits, what you leave behind, and where you head next.

LODESTAR

How do you let go of guilt, regret, and shame? Here are three strategies that can transform your relationship with all three emotions:

- **Reframe the narrative.** We all have narratives about who we are. What we don't always realize is that we have an opportunity to rewrite them whenever and however we choose. If you've been wrapped up in a tired narrative that's tethering you to guilt, regret, or shame, it's time to untangle yourself. You can't change what's already happened to you, but it isn't what happened that matters; it's how you respond.

- **Turn pain into potential, and shame into action.** Looking backward will never move you forward. As long as your mind keeps playing your "lowlight reel" on loop, you'll stay stuck in the past. Instead, use moments of great pain or loss as powerful catalysts to make a difference.

- **Own your shame—and share it.** Shame loves to dwell in the shadows. If you shine a light on it and claim it as part of your story, it loses its power. If you feel guilty, be honest. If you're filled with regret, be vulnerable. If you feel shame about something, take it public. The more you can coax shame out of the dark, the less hold it has over you.

....

CHAPTER 6

CULTIVATE RESILIENCE: BOUNCING BACK FROM ADVERSITY, REJECTION, AND FAILURE

If you're constantly pushing yourself higher and higher, the law of averages predicts that you will at some point fall. And when you do, I want you to remember this: There is no such thing as failure. Failure is just life trying to move us in another direction.

—OPRAH WINFREY

WHAT DO YOU DO WHEN THE GOING GETS TOUGH?

From time to time, we find ourselves in a moment of crisis, or suffering at the hands of yet another rejection, or weathering eras that seem to be marked by failure. These challenges make us question our ability to overcome the obstacles ahead. It can feel impossible to see a way through. So, in an effort to avoid the discomfort that comes part and parcel with adversity, we avoid it at all costs. But the hard truth is that we can handle it—and we're often much better when we do.

There's a dangerous myth that is virtually endemic in today's society, and it hampers happiness, success, and growth. The myth tells us that we are inherently fragile and that the only way to be happy and successful is to protect ourselves from adversity—life's difficulties or misfortunes. Not only is that belief false but the actions we take to evade adversity, rejection, and failure usually limit our happiness—and even stifle personal and professional growth. Those who play the game of life not to lose seldom ever really win.

While it's wise to guard ourselves and our families from "clear and present dangers," we have a tendency to overprotect. According to two important books on the subject—*The Coddling of the American Mind* by Greg Lukianoff and Jonathan Haidt and *A Nation of Wimps* by Hara Estroff Marano—overprotection is the greatest failure a society can commit. It engenders a victim mentality and a false belief in fragility, all while hindering growth.

Why do we choose to avoid the hard stuff, if the greatest opportunities for growth await us on the other side?

Blame it on our brains. Psychologically, we're wired to avoid pain and discomfort. But when we acknowledge that adversity is par for the course—and that it's often necessary for growth—we open ourselves up to the many benefits that come with challenging circumstances.

WHY IS BOUNCING BACK SO IMPORTANT?

Rather than trying to avoid all adversity—an impossible feat—we should accept the inevitability of adversity and the occasional crises in life and prepare for them. As the body's muscles grow stronger with stress, so can people, teams, organizations, and even communities.

This is a particularly vital insight—one so valuable that George has spent much of his career studying it. While others had surmised that some people were simply built to be resilient while others were not, George and his colleagues found that anyone can build resilience and reap its myriad benefits. That is, if they focus on the right factors. His book on the subject, *Stronger: Develop the Resilience You Need to Succeed*, explores the ways in which resilient people address adversity and recover from setbacks. With that in mind, let's talk about how it's done, so that you can take a page from his book (and ours, of course).

Never Let a Good Crisis Go to Waste

At the dawn of the twentieth century, the written form of the Chinese language largely changed to the logo-syllabic Mandarin form, which uses symbols to capture a writer's intention. The English word "crisis" is captured by two symbols: one for "danger" and the other for "possibility." Crises reveal true strength. They also serve as opportunities for those prepared to take advantage of them. As Rahm Emanuel, one of President Obama's key advisers, once noted, "You never let a serious crisis go to waste. And what I mean by that is it's an opportunity to do things you think you could not do before."

History provides countless examples of leaders who overcame great challenges to become the remarkable figures we know today. John Steinbeck once said, "We give the President more work than a man can do, more responsibility than a man should take, more pressure than a man can bear." American presidential leadership is a master class in leadership under stress. It teaches us powerful lessons about effectiveness and ineffectiveness in times of crisis as well as how great leaders can cultivate unification and growth from the seeds of adversity.

C-SPAN has collected survey data on the effectiveness of presidents for over two decades. The organization found one of the most critical predictors of leadership effectiveness overall is the ability to guide through a crisis. It's been said that a rising tide lifts all boats, but only the most seaworthy can withstand the storm, while others sink in the roiling and violent waters of turmoil. Put simply: it's easy to lead when things are going well, but true leaders emerge in times of adversity. C-SPAN found that the most effective presidential leaders overall were also the best leaders in times of crisis, ultimately unifying diverse people and strengthening our collective sense of community.

Who were C-SPAN's standouts? George Washington's transformative leadership contributed to the creation of a new nation. Abraham Lincoln saved that nation and set into motion actions that would allow it to become stronger than ever before. Theodore Roosevelt resolved a crippling mining crisis in 1902 and in doing so gave new status to the American labor movement. He was also the driving force behind the creation of the National Parks Service. Finally, Franklin D. Roosevelt's policies saved the nation twice. Once from a paralyzing financial crisis in 1933 by implementing policies that continue even today to provide stability, support, and growth, and once again from the threats of megalomaniacal foreign dictators in the 1940s.

What has history and current research taught us about the secrets of transformative, resilient presidential leadership? There are five key elements (each of which George details in his book *Leading beyond Crisis*), which we can remember with the mnemonic OPTIC:

1. Optimistic vision/agenda
2. Performance (decisiveness and action)
3. Tenacity
4. Integrity
5. Collaboration

OPTIC can help us better understand the failures or successes of all types of leaders at all levels—city, state, national, or organizational. We can also use this transformative lens to better choose our leaders in the future and to become better leaders ourselves.

Find Power in the Pain

But it's important to remember that it's not just how you handle a crisis that makes you a great leader; simply enduring hardships equips you with the strength to go further than you may have thought possible.

Faced with chronic depression, political failure, and the loss of a son, Lincoln rose from the ashes of failure and tragedy to become a transformational leader. By putting the lessons he learned from coping with monumental personal and professional challenges to use, he became one of the greatest and most beloved American presidents of all time.

Grade-school teachers believed that Thomas Edison was "too stupid to learn anything." Later in life, after failing thousands of times in his quest to create a light bulb filament that would light and burn consistently, he invented the world's first practical incandescent light bulb. When asked by a reporter what it felt like to endure so many failures, Edison replied, "I didn't fail 1,000 times. The light bulb was an invention with 1,000 steps."

After he was ousted from Apple, Steve Jobs eventually regained control of the company and went on to create the world's most recognized brand and its largest tech company by revenue. That first rejection ultimately spurred incredible success.

Famed chocolatier Milton Hershey grew up in poverty due to his father's penchant for get-rich-quick schemes—from cough drop sales to consignment ventures across America. When he was fourteen, Milton began working at Royer's Ice Cream Parlor in Lancaster, Pennsylvania. He eventually took his talents in flavor development to the candymaking side of the business, where he found himself to be a talented confectioner.

Growing up, Milton expected to give up his part-time passion project to work in manual labor and care for his family—but the joy he found in creating and selling sweets followed him to every job, from newspaper apprenticing to farmhand work. Eventually, Milton followed his gift and took out a bank loan to begin the Lancaster Caramel Company.

After a decade of great success, he acquired a dairy farm hoping to develop a recipe for milk chocolate (a luxury few could afford at the time) to bring to the public. Milton sold his caramel business and, after a series of failed attempts, produced the first Hersey's Milk Chocolate Bar in 1900. He established the Hershey Company, and the rest, as they say, is history. Today, Hershey rakes in an annual revenue of $1.5 billion and remains one of the leading confectionery companies in the world.

Where would our culture be today if some of our greatest leaders and innovators had not found the fortitude to keep going— even when the world was telling them to stop? Rather than fear the possibility of failure, or give up entirely after being knocked down, they used their setbacks and demonstrated the resilience necessary to try—and try again.

Adversity as a means of making great strides is well documented in science and psychology. For instance, in their 2012 study of Olympic gold medal winners, sports psychologists David Fletcher and Mustafa Sarkar found that adversity and resilience were actually key to the Olympians' success. As they explain, "Most of the participants argued that if they had not experienced certain types of stressors at specific times, including highly demanding adversities...they would not have won their gold medals." And it's not just limited to the world's highest achievers.

In 1995, psychologists Richard Tedeschi and Lawrence Calhoun coined the term "post-traumatic growth," which they described as the experience of positive change resulting from highly challenging life crises. They identified this phenomenon in everyday people who had survived very difficult things: "Bereavement, rheumatoid arthritis, HIV infection, cancer, bone marrow transplantation, heart attacks, coping with the medical problems of children, transportation accidents, house fires, sexual assault and sexual abuse, combat, refugee experiences, and being taken hostage," to name just a few.[15] Their post-traumatic growth came in numerous forms, including an increased appreciation for life in general, more meaningful interpersonal relationships, an increased sense of personal strength, changed priorities, and a richer existential and spiritual life.

You, too, have the power to reach unimaginable heights by weathering adversity, rejection, and failure—and resolving to do better next time. In fact, we believe failure in particular should be a cause for celebration.

Celebrate Your Worst Ideas

Over at the 1-800-Flowers headquarters, there's a special corner with a name you might find surprising: "Jim's Wall of Shame." For every success 1-800-Flowers has celebrated, there have been plenty of ideas that missed the mark—sometimes to the point that laughter was the only appropriate response.

Years ago on a visit to Boston's Quincy Market, Jim stopped by the stall of a vendor named Lucy. Lucy loved a theme. She owned several specialty shops in the area. One was called Lucy's Heart, and everything was emblazoned with a heart; at Lucy's Rainbow, every item for sale featured—you guessed it—a rainbow; and so on. That sparked something for Jim: *I bet we can sell anything with a flower on it!* he thought.

Back at work, Jim rallied his team around a new offering: a catalog of unique gifts, each linked to his business with a flower of some kind. That included a particular item Jim was excited about—a set of beautiful silk jackets, each embroidered with an intricate rose on the back. By the end of the quarter, the catalog had proven to be a colossal failure, with Jim's jackets an especially big flop. Not a single one sold (in fact, if you're interested, he can get you a great deal on one of 'em).

After coming to terms with the fact that customers wanted fresh flowers on demand, not elegant outerwear, the team tacked up one of those jackets as the focal point on what would become the Wall of Shame. In years since, the wall has grown to include many other failed ideas—Jim's and others'. The wall is a source of humor, sure, but there's a deeper meaning there. Jim encourages new team members to earn their way onto the wall—to fail and fail big. Why?

Failing early (and often) not only strengthens resilience but also builds within us a mental barometer for making smarter decisions. Failure is key for growth in both our personal and professional lives, which makes it a cause for celebration. Something better is inevitably coming. The trick is not to wallow too long. Laugh, let it go, and move on.

What if you're having trouble finding the humor in your latest blunder? Imagine it happened to a friend. If you can laugh at their misstep—or simply offer words of encouragement and help them shake it off—you can do the same for yourself.

Turn Failure into Opportunity

Do you remember the day the Coca-Cola Company announced its new formula?

It was the spring of 1985—April 23 to be exact. Coca-Cola's sales had been slipping over the previous fifteen years as it slowly lost market share to its primary competitor. The company thought it would shake things up in hopes of increasing consumer preference and awareness, both of which had gone downhill alongside sales.

Coca-Cola had done its research, testing its updated concoction with nearly two hundred thousand consumers. It was with great excitement that it announced the formula had been revitalized, marking the first adjustment to the recipe in ninety-nine years. But buyers were not thrilled. Actually, they were outraged.

Suddenly, nostalgia for the old formula reached a fever pitch, with people protesting in droves, writing rude letters to the CEO (one was addressed to "Chief Dodo"), flooding the hotline with angry calls, and stockpiling bottles and cans with the original formula.

But what else were they doing? Talking about Coke in ways they hadn't for more than a decade. The switch made people realize just how important the beverage was to them. And that was a huge, unexpected benefit.

When Coke announced it was bringing back the original formula, to be labeled "Coca-Cola Classic," the world rejoiced. It was front-page news, and no one was happier than the hoards of consumers who had lamented the change. Ultimately, what was seen as one of the biggest blunders in consumer goods history became one of its largest boons, boosting customer loyalty and giving Coke an additional product line to market with its own distinct campaign. It's evidence that what doesn't kill you can indeed make you much, much stronger. Failure, rejection, adversity—they're all opportunities. The question is what you'll do with them.

Transform for a Better Tomorrow

Jim's friend Mike Milken knows this all too well. He launched his career by spotting an untapped opportunity. In a postgrad course at Wharton, he began studying bonds. His research led him to a remarkable discovery.

Companies that had once held blue-chip status were downgraded from AAA to C (or "junk") status when things got rough for them. But those ratings were only indicative of how they had performed in the past, not what they might do in the future. As a result, they were very cheap. That meant they posed immense opportunity—if investors were willing to gamble on them.[16] After graduating from Wharton, Mike took a job as a trader at Drexel Firestone. His task was to research low-grade bonds. In the years that followed, the company went through several mergers, and along the way Mike asked about opening a high-yield bond department. His supervisors agreed and offered him a small amount of funds to start it up. Within a few short years, he was earning 100 percent on that money.

The high-yield market skyrocketed. But eventually, things took a turn. In 1989, Mike was indicted for racketeering and securities fraud, pleading guilty to securities and reporting violations. He was sentenced to ten years in prison, in addition to incurring steep fines and a permanent ban from the securities industry by the SEC. But he didn't let that stop him from doing good.

Mike had always been committed to supporting the causes important to him: medical advancements, education, and public health. After his release from prison (he served two years due to his willingness to cooperate with authorities and good behavior), he reinvested his time and resources in philanthropy. He has supported strides in medical research, education, and public health through the Milken Family Foundation, an organization dedicated to increasing educational opportunity, which he founded in 1982; the Milken Institute—an economic think tank hosting hundreds of conferences and events; George Washington University's Milken Institute School of Public Health; and the soon-to-launch Milken Center for Advancing the American Dream, which has the goal of "advancing economic and social mobility for all," to name just a handful of his efforts.[17] He and his wife, Lori, are members of the Giving Pledge, "a promise by the world's wealthiest individuals and families to dedicate the majority of their wealth to charitable causes."[18]

From granting funds to medical researchers digging into cures for various forms of cancer, to recognizing America's best teachers and funding mentorship opportunities for exceptional high school students facing hardship, Mike understands that we can't change the past, but we have control over how we show up today, tomorrow, and the day after that.

Senior Associate Dean for Leadership Studies and the Lester Crown Professor in the Practice of Management at Yale School of Management Jeffrey Sonnenfeld's book *Firing Back: How Great Leaders Rebound after Career Disasters* demonstrates the impact of letting go of the past and committing to the future. He and coauthor Andrew Ward analyzed more than 450 successions at publicly traded companies over the course of four years and found that only 35 percent of CEOs who had been let go took on another executive role within two years of their ousting.[19]

"What prevents a deposed leader from coming back?" they write. "Leaders who cannot recover have a tendency to blame themselves and are often tempted to dwell on the past rather than look to the future. They secretly hold themselves responsible for their career setback, whether they were or not, and get caught in a psychological web of their own making, unable to move beyond the position they no longer hold."

What about those who do recover? According to Sonnenfeld and Ward, they essentially follow Joseph Campbell's "hero's myth." They interviewed three hundred CEOs and other professionals and found that, to recover, "they must carefully *decide how to fight back*. Once this crucial decision has been taken, they must *recruit others into battle*. They must then *take steps to recover their heroic status,* in the process proving to themselves and others that they have the *mettle* necessary to *rediscover their heroic mission.*"

The first step is deciding whether or not to confront what happened. Sometimes, the answer is letting go. They share the example of Home Depot cofounder Bernie Marcus. In 1978, Marcus "decided to sidestep the quicksand of litigation against Sigoloff, and the conglomerate that fired Marcus from Handy Dan Home Improvement. Marcus made his battleground the market-place rather than the courtroom. Thanks to this strategy, he was free to set the historic course for Home Depot," which has more than $157 billion in annual revenue.[20]

Our friend Jamie Dimon also chose the high road when he was asked to leave his position as president of Citigroup by then-chairman Sandy Weill after sixteen years of partnership, choosing to go without a fight. In fact, a year later, Dimon asked to meet with Weill and thank him for all he'd done for Jamie. By letting go and moving forward, "he was able to turn his ouster into an event that yielded both helpful perspective and reassuring resolution."[21] The rest, as they say, is history.

Tap into Vision and Tenacity

Let's say adversity, rejection, or failure is knocking at your door. Things are bad, and you know you need to do something to move on. How can you harness your circumstances to improve your station?

There are two traits that predict your ability to bounce back. The first is having a positive vision of yourself and the future. You have to believe you're capable of bouncing back. But the journey doesn't stop there. In the hundreds of psychological case studies

George has conducted, a key secondary element is present in nearly all participants who manage to reckon with a plan gone awry: tenacity.

Tenacity is the elbow grease necessary to bring that vision to life. A woman we'll call Kathleen serves as a powerful example. Kathleen was raised in a terribly abusive home. Despite the hardship of her early years, she held on to her vision for a better life and went on to graduate from college. From there, she set her sights on graduate school, and her hard work paid off: she was admitted to her dream program.

But then Kathleen got pregnant. Without financial or familial support, she was forced to drop out and raise her child as a single mother. Unable to pay rent, Kathleen lost her housing and wound up living on a boat. Not just any boat—one with a hole in it.

Every morning, Kathleen had to quite literally bail herself out to keep her home from sinking altogether. But in the midst of great challenge—a time when most people would have given up entirely, Kathleen held tight to her belief that a better life was waiting for her.

In the meantime, she did whatever it took to keep herself and her child afloat. In the evenings, she'd dress up and head to local hotels, because she knew they'd be hosting one function or another. There, she'd hit the buffet tables, stuffing her pockets and purse so she and her child could eat.

Despite these circumstances, Kathleen knew that it was possible to create a better life. Just as she had escaped the terrible home life of her early years, she knew it would take clear vision and determination to find her way. Kathleen did just that, going on to earn a PhD and become extremely successful in her field.

At the outset, your vision doesn't have to be detailed. Really, all it takes is a belief that something better is destined for you and that you have the grit and tenacity to make that destiny your reality.

Another unlikely example of vision and tenacity embodied? Anthony Scaramucci, whom you may know from his brief stint on Capitol Hill.

Scaramucci was wildly embarrassed when he was fired from his role as White House communications director just ten days after starting the job. He had messed up big time, calling *New Yorker* Washington correspondent Ryan Lizza to find out who had leaked information about a private dinner the reporter had tweeted about. On the call, he speculated about who might have provided the tip and his plans to fire various staff members. But what he didn't do was say the call was "off the record." Lizza published exactly what Scaramucci had said.

It wasn't the end of his public missteps. The crypto exchange FTX acquired 30 percent of SkyBridge Capital, the alternative investment firm Scaramucci founded, in late 2022—just prior to FTX's myriad fraud charges and ultimate collapse. But "the Mooch" knows fame is valuable, even if it's infamy. And he used that knowledge to get back on his feet.

While others would cower in shame, Scaramucci followed up the crypto exchange snafu with an appearance on *Special Forces: World's Toughest Test*, a television show in which celebrities face physical challenges from the Special Forces selection process. He has a positive vision and he's willing to do whatever it takes to achieve it, even if it seems embarrassing or lowbrow. That kind of tenacity is hard to come by, but if you can cultivate it, you can weather almost any storm.

LESSONS FROM THE BEST SELF-HELP BOOKS ON BOUNCING BACK FROM ADVERSITY, REJECTION, AND FAILURE

Man's Search for Meaning by **Viktor Frankl**

Originally published in 1946, *Man's Search for Meaning* details the harrowing experiences of author and psychologist Viktor Frankl during his internment in Auschwitz concentration camp during World War II. The powerful memoir offers insight into how we can survive unsurvivable situations, come to terms with trauma, and ultimately find meaning amid the unimaginable.

In the years that followed the camp's liberation in 1945, Frankl shares, "The way in which a man accepts his fate and all the suffering it entails, the way in which he takes up his cross, gives him ample opportunity—even under the most difficult circumstances—to add a deeper meaning to his life." Frankl shares the importance of "mental courage" through hardship, and the importance of holding out hope for a better life on the other side of the struggle. He offers the following vital insights:

- Decisions, not conditions, determine who we are and what we will become.
- A positive outlook is a gift we can each give ourselves, and no one can take it away—no matter their power over us. "Our greatest freedom is the freedom to choose our attitude."
- When a way forward on a chosen path feels impassable, think of it as an opportunity for transformation and growth. "When we are no longer able to change a situation, we are challenged to change ourselves."

- Frankl writes, "Between stimulus and response, there is a space. In that space is our power to choose our response. In our response lies our growth and our freedom."

The Celestine Prophecy: An Adventure by James Redfield

James Redfield's 1993 novel *The Celestine Prophecy* chronicles an unnamed narrator's spiritual awakening and his quest to find a Peruvian manuscript that, if deciphered, would reveal the ancient mysteries that govern the world. On this journey, he discovers the power of synchronicity, or the belief that coincidences aren't merely happenstance and instead hold special significance in our lives.

Speaking to the importance of embracing the unknown, and the growth and possibility that often accompanies it, Redfield's narrator shares, "Fear lowers one's vibration tremendously." As the novel reveals, when we eliminate the margin for risk in our lives, we lose out completely on the wisdom and potential success that just might come our way following outright failure.

Redfield makes a case for the adage "the only way is through," and champions the wisdom that comes from the wins and losses of every hero's journey. As he explains, "we must assume every event has significance and contains a message that pertains to our questions. This especially applies to what we used to call bad things. The challenge is to find the silver lining in every event, no matter how negative."

What I Know for Sure by Oprah Winfrey

Rejection and failure sting, no doubt about that, shares Oprah in her 2014 bestselling memoir *What I Know for Sure*. But she teaches that the life you dream of can be yours—regardless of the challenges you encounter—with equal parts self-belief and grit (sounds a lot like positive vision and tenacity, doesn't it?).

Born in 1954 in Kosciusko, Mississippi, Oprah Gail Winfrey (originally spelled Orpah) was raised in poverty and faced abuse throughout her adolescence. Despite a childhood marred by adversity and trauma, Oprah held tight to the belief that a greater life awaited her. Turning struggle into strength helped her go from interviewing corncob dolls (since her family couldn't afford Barbies) to becoming one of the most beloved media titans the world has ever seen—and having a Barbie created in her likeness.

On the peaks and valleys of her life, Oprah shares, "Whenever I'm faced with a difficult decision, I ask myself: *What would I do if I weren't afraid of making a mistake, feeling rejected, looking foolish, or being alone?* I know for sure that when you remove the fear, the answer you've been searching for comes into focus. And as you walk into what you fear, you should know for sure that your deepest struggle can, if you're willing and open, produce your greatest strength." Whether it's a win or a loss, what matters most is that we muster the courage to try.

When it comes to struggle, it's essential that we let the obstacles we face serve as our teachers. Resilience is key to allowing ourselves to learn from these lessons, not repeat the same mistakes, and make our way further, in ways large and small, toward our purpose. In *What I Know for Sure*, Oprah assures us that:

- Self-belief can be fostered through faith, be it in a higher power or in oneself—and trusting the process and appreciating the journey is key. Oprah advises, "Say 'Thank You' because your faith is so strong that you don't doubt that whatever the problem, you'll get through it."

- "No matter what challenge you may be facing, you must remember that while the canvas of your life is painted with daily experiences, behaviors, reactions, and emotions, you're the one controlling the brush. If I had known this at 21, I could have saved myself a lot of heartache and self-doubt. It would have been a revelation to understand that we are all the artists of our own lives—and that we can use as many colors and brushstrokes as we like."
- The first step to achieving a dream? Take it out of your mind and into your hands. Don't wait until a more convenient time. Be bold and make the first move to begin your journey. Trust your inner magic to guide your way. "Whatever you can do, or dream you can, begin it. Boldness has genius, power, and magic in it."

RISING ABOVE CIRCUMSTANCE WITH DR. BEN CARSON

Neuroscientist and former American presidential candidate Dr. Ben Carson might seem like the kind of person who faced few setbacks in life, but that's just not so. Growing up in Detroit, Carson made poor marks in his early years, lived on food stamps, and witnessed those he loved most face severe mental health struggles.

At the age of five, after his mother discovered that his father had another family from a previous marriage, Ben's mother attempted suicide and underwent a series of hospitalizations for psychiatric treatment.

During that time, the emotional turmoil within his family and other changes caused Carson to lag behind other students. Dr. Carson transitioned from a public school to a two-classroom setting, and in this new environment, a significant portion of time was devoted to singing songs and playing games rather than focused learning. In Carson's words, he "essentially lost a year of school."

After his mother left his father, she became the primary bread-winner of the family and picked up on her young son's struggling academics. She began limiting the time he spent in front of the television and asked Carson to read and write two reports on books from the library per week. This taught young Ben the practice of quiet, dedicated study, and he managed to catch up to his brightest classmates and earn top marks.

Carson set his sights on becoming a doctor after seeing the lavish lifestyles they seemed to lead on the television dramas of the day. He continued to excel academically and participated in a variety of extracurricular activities, including band, chess club, and the US Army Junior Reserve Officers' Training Corps (JROTC) program, where he reached the highest rank of cadet colonel.

Carson graduated third in his class and earned degrees from Yale University and the Johns Hopkins University School of Medicine's neurosurgery program, establishing himself as a leader in the field as a neurosurgeon specializing in traumatic brain injuries, brain and spinal tumors, and neurological disorders. Several of his operations on conjoined twins were among the first in the field and contributed to the advancement of separation research.

George had an opportunity to sit down with Dr. Carson to query him on how he handled the potential for failure in neurosurgery. He asked him, "How do you know when to perform a surgery that no one else has done, versus walking away from it?"

Carson shared that, in both low-stakes and high-stress operations, he used a very simple matrix: "What's the best thing that happens if I don't, and what's the worst thing that happens if I do?" Over the years, he's made some gutsy decisions with these prompting questions. Ultimately, negative outcomes are possible in any circumstance, but this risk assessment can apply to nearly any choice we're asked to make.

As Carson explains, exact certainty is seldom a guarantee in life. What we are called to do, to the best of our abilities, is consider each potential outcome and determine which will best suit our given situation. Recognize what we are capable of (or what is truly within our power to control) and lead with confidence knowing that, no matter the result, we've made a well-informed choice.

LODESTAR

When things are looking down, tell yourself there's nowhere to go but up. But how do you do that when things are feeling particularly bleak?

- **Remind yourself that the best opportunities lie in crisis.** Remember Rahm Emanuel's wise words: "You never let a serious crisis go to waste." When things go wrong, you're looking at your best opportunity to turn things around and make them trend in the opposite direction.

- **Cultivate resilience's two key ingredients.** Resilience is built on two key ingredients: positive vision and tenacity. Believe you can get where you want to go and put in the work to make it there. Those efforts will help you navigate the choppiest of waters.

- **Don't forget that you have agency, even in your darkest hour.** Reflect on Viktor Frankl's vital insight: decisions, not conditions, determine who we are and what we'll become.

....

CHAPTER 7

YOUR RÉSUMÉ IS A VERB: BECOMING A LIFELONG LEARNER

Anyone who stops learning is old, whether at twenty
or eighty. Anyone who keeps learning stays young.

—Henry Ford

"What accomplishments are still on your bucket list?"
Jim posed the question to five of his buddies over dinner one night. Every member had achieved quite a lot by any stretch of the imagination. But they readily took their turns, each ticking off item after item—skills and competencies they had yet to conquer. Clearly, they had done some thinking on the subject. The question is one that most highly successful people have answers for,

along with many others that drive them to continue pushing the envelope:

How can I be more knowledgeable?

How can I advance my skills?

How can I encounter new experiences and challenges?

They know that true progress has no finish line.

"Your résumé is a verb" is a statement Jim has been making for years to encourage the people in his life—family, friends, and colleagues—to ask themselves questions like those. Of course, "résumé" is a noun (according to George's beloved *Oxford English Dictionary*, at least). But referring to it as a verb serves as a little cognitive speed bump that encourages you to slow down and think about what you're doing to keep advancing the ball today, tomorrow, and for the rest of your life. Those of us who are in constant pursuit of something more—of doing and being better than we are today—are always willing to do what it takes to get to the next level. And that means we're primed to keep getting better, even when we're well past what society might consider to be our "prime."

Why Is Viewing Your Résumé as a Verb So Important?

If you accept the notion that your résumé is a noun, a retrospective of sorts, quite frankly, it's over. The journey is done once a particular role, or even your career at large, ends, and you're merely an accountant adding up the events of your life. But if you see that résumé as a verb, something that's always moving—always changing—you're still on the path, and new opportunities lie around every corner.

What does living as if your résumé as a verb look like in real life? Imagine you're planning the next vacation. You have the option to head to a Caribbean island, lie on the beach, crack open a cooler of beer, and contemplate your navel for a week. Or you could book a trip to a small city in Spain, which would give you the chance to dust off the Spanish you haven't used since high school. It would be slightly uncomfortable, since you haven't practiced it in so long, but you'd have the chance to take a cooking class and prepare a beautiful paella—something you'd been wanting to try for years. Which choice cultivates that résumé, forcing you to step outside your comfort zone in search of growth, even in your free time?

We've tried to push our children and grandchildren toward the latter, asking them the questions we hoped they would eventually ask themselves. So now, we'll ask you:

What have you learned today?

Where are you volunteering?

What are you listening to?

What are you doing to improve your physical health?

What have you taught yourself this year?

Often, it's after you graduate from a traditional school environment that the real learning and fun start. Everything you do offers the opportunity to make yourself smarter, more knowledgeable, more valuable, and better rounded—if you put in the work to make it happen.

Hack Your Mind

To get into the science behind lifelong learning, we sat down with Dr. Daniel Willingham, a cognitive scientist, educator, and author known for his research on how the brain works and how people learn. A professor of psychology at the University of Virginia, Dr. Willingham has written numerous articles and books on topics such as cognitive psychology, education, and literacy, including

Outsmart Your Brain: Why Learning Is Hard and How You Can Make It Easy.

According to Dr. Willingham, learners of any age can use their minds as tools to retain more than they ever thought possible. The key? When you know how the brain acquires new information, you can hack it to work in your favor.

For example, attention is a critical component of learning. The human brain is naturally inclined to focus on things that are relevant and interesting. If you can design learning experiences that capture your attention and make the process fun and engaging, you're more likely to retain that information. Storytelling, hands-on activities, and multimedia help us keep interest and focus. It's why social media is so compelling.

But often we scroll right through new information in search of the next shiny thing and forget it right after we see it. How do you remember the stuff that matters? According to Dr. Willingham, repetition and practice can go a long way in helping you retain it. If it's important to hold on to, make sure you're making the time to reflect on what you've learned and practice any corresponding skills to make them stick.

What if you'd rather lie on a beach and drink a cold one than engage in the challenge involved in exploring unfamiliar territory? It's time to check in with your motivation. We're all driven by different things; think about what makes you tick and why you get out of bed in the morning. Then, attempt to connect that new material to your interests and goals. You'll be that much more likely to pursue the road less traveled.

Lean into Learning Relationships

George has received numerous unusual opportunities over the course of his life. When people ask, "How did you get the chance to do *that*?" or the slightly ruder, "Why did they pick you?" they usually don't like the answer. Nine times out of ten, he just wanted to learn something. He did his research, found out who was the best at it in the world—or in the country, at the very least—and showed up at their door.

"Look, you don't know me," he often found himself saying, "but I've read your stuff. I'm really interested in what you're doing, so interested that I'll work for free." He approached them with sincerity and humility, and he found that they were almost always willing to do whatever they could to help a guy out. They became teachers, and close friends, who would have a lifelong impact—particularly when he made the effort to stay in touch well after their work together ended.

Jim has seen the power of maintaining those relationships too. More than two decades ago, he was at an investor conference in Aspen, Colorado. He and his wife were at a beautiful mountaintop dinner, seated with eight other people—strangers who would soon become friends. A woman at the table asked each person to share a story about a teacher who had a meaningful impact on their life. Jim described a history professor at John Jay College of Criminal Justice and the difference she had made for him.

"Are you talking about Blanche Cook?" the woman asked.

Jim was startled. "How did you know?"

"Well," the woman said, "the way you were talking about her—Blanche is one of my best friends."

After Jim finished his story about Professor Cook, the woman asked, "Have you ever told Blanche that?"

His answer, embarrassingly enough, was no. But now he had a chance to change that.

He went out of his way to find Blanche, sit down with her over a cup of coffee, and tell her about the impact she had made on his life. They have been close ever since. When she retired in March of 2023 after fifty-three years of teaching, Jim sent her a letter that her partner, Claire, read at her retirement party, along with a big bouquet of flowers. The attendees learned about the impact she continues to have on students who have long left the classroom.

Mind the Company You Keep

Over the years, Jim would find himself in other classrooms, taking on the role of instructor himself—all while learning from students and their teachers.

For a number of years, Jim has been invited to speak to Professor Jeffrey Sonnenfeld's class at Yale and have lunch with its participants. It's the kind of occasion that makes you want to go back to school—connecting with smart and engaged students preparing to be the next generation of movers and shakers in business. Everyone gets something out of it. The students get to learn from Jim's extensive leadership experience in the business world, and Jim gets to learn about the trends and opportunities holding their attention and participate in the CEO forums Jeffrey cultivates as part of this initiative.

Over the years, Jim's organization has connected with hundreds of Yalies who continue to share their insights on the latest business topics and even provide feedback on what 1-800-Flowers is doing. Hanging around with smart, assertive, thoughtful people keeps

you in the flow. It makes you better. And when you make cultivating those kinds of relationships an ongoing pursuit, you can't
help but learn for the long haul.

In 2023, Jim had the opportunity to learn about Jeffrey and the
students' work to get companies to withdraw their business from
Russia after Putin invaded Ukraine.[22] Jeffrey has been committed
to corporate social responsibility since the beginning of his career,
founding the Chief Executive Leadership at Yale, and advocating
for CEOs to take a stand on gun control, voting rights, and more.
With that in mind, he and his students began keeping a public
list of companies that had ended their relationship with Russia.
His research team updated the list hourly, watching it grow by the
hundreds to include BP, Shell, ExxonMobil, McKinsey, Bain, BCG,
IBM, Dell, Meta, Apple, and Alphabet, among many others.[23]

And in doing so, he and his team inadvertently built a community of "CEOs [who] wanted to be seen as doing the right thing...It
was a rare unity of patriotic mission, personal values, genuine
concern for world peace, and corporate self-interest."[24] It's further
proof that surrounding yourself with the right people really does
make a difference.

Say No to Jerks

Chief Executive Leadership Institute Legend in Leadership
awardee Ron Shaich agrees. In an interview with Jim McCann, the
managing partner and CEO of Act III Holdings, a $1-billion-plus
fund investing in restaurant and consumer companies; chairman
of fast-casual restaurant Cava; founder and former chairman and
CEO of Panera Bread; and founder of Au Bon Pain says, "The good
of the many is always more important than the good of the few."

A key tenet of his leadership approach? "No jerks."

That was number one on Panera's list of cultural values during his tenure. According to Shaich, it means that "our relationships with each other and with our guests are based on respect and honesty, and they establish a standard for our conduct."[25]

As he explains, "'No jerks' does not mean we agree on everything. It means we listen, we discuss and debate, we consider different viewpoints, we find common ground, and we move forward in a way that benefits our business, which, in turn, benefits [all stakeholders]."[26]

His "no jerks" policy included speaking out about the importance of condemning hatred and standing up for what's right after a series of hate-based events around the country in 2017, including the white nationalist rally that took place in Charlottesville, Virginia, in August of that year. Shaich wrote to his team, "I don't think there's ever been a more important time for us to stand up as citizens for our American values and voice our disgust for hate based on race, religion, gender, or sexual orientation. You can count me personally as one American who will do all in my power to fight hate. And within Panera, there's never been a more important time for us to live our Cultural Value of respecting the dignity of the whole person, the differences in people and the diversity they bring to our team, our cafes, and our communities. I am very proud that Panera has always been a place where all law-abiding people are welcome to work, to eat, and to gather without intimidation, and you can rest assured your entire leadership team is committed to keeping it that way."[27]

Panera's success was because of, rather than in spite of, Shaich's dedication to the collective good. With Shaich at the helm, Panera produced "annualized returns in excess of 25 percent over the last two decades of [his] tenure and delivered a total shareholder return 44 times better than the S&P 500 from July 18, 1997, to July 18, 2017 (when Ron led a $7.8 billion sale of Panera in what is the largest US restaurant deal at among the highest multiples—18x EBITDA—on record)." [28]

Find Teachers in Unexpected Places

Our best teachers aren't always found in the classroom. You already know about Jim's first job at St. John's Home for Boys in Queens. There, he was thrown into the fire time after time and got to be pretty good at it as he moved up the ranks. Eventually, he was overseeing a staff of hundreds working shifts around the clock to take care of boys in different facilities—everyone from cooks to maintenance people, counselors, and psychiatrists. Of course, he couldn't do it entirely on his own.

At twenty-four, he met a wonderful woman who was to be his "assistant," Jane Garrity. She lived in Rockaway, Queens, just a few blocks from one of the facilities—a two-block building seated directly on the beach.

The truth is, while Jim was technically in charge, Jane ran the show. Being the wonderful person she was, she let him believe he was really making the decisions. She taught without lecturing, encouraging him to see things from a different perspective—all while ensuring that everything that needed to get done got done the right way. And she absolutely bamboozled him into thinking he had figured it all out on his own! They worked together for more than ten years and stayed in touch for the rest of Jane's life.

The last day he saw her was November 12, 2001, just two months after 9/11. An American Airlines plane had crashed into the Rockaway Peninsula shortly after takeoff, killing all 260 people on board and five people on the ground. Jim's sister lived near the crash—just a few blocks from Jane—so Jim and his brother rushed down to make sure everyone was OK. As they turned onto Jane's block, they saw an engine smoldering in the street.

When Jane answered the door, she and Jim just hugged for a few minutes, and then she invited him and his brother in for a cup of tea. She died not long after.

Looking back, he was grateful for that last goodbye. Jane had taught him so much about how to be a grown-up, and she didn't make him feel stupid when he did something silly along the way. Most importantly, she helped him understand how to teach himself.

Ride the Waves

When it comes to learning, how you seek out information—and put effort into your own evolution—is just as important as finding great teachers. At 1-800-Flowers.com, everyone knows their role is to be a cultural engineer, regardless of what it says in their job description. It's the culture—inside and out—that makes the company what it is, and we learn from it by what we choose to celebrate and what we choose to ignore or punish.

For the Flowers team, the focus on culture and global progress has led to five waves of development. The first wave was marked by stores—one and then many more.

The second wave ushered in a new primary access modality, the 800 number, with a name change to match: from Flora Plenty to 1-800-Flowers. In half a dozen years, 1-800-Flowers became the prominent brand in its category by embracing new technology when everyone else said it wouldn't work.

With that, the team made the commitment to keep their antennae up, always looking for new technology so they could be the disruptor as opposed to the other way around. The company embarked on more than fifty technology experiments. Many of them, such as catalogs on CD-ROMs, never panned out, but a little platform called the World Wide Web did. The third wave came when Flowers decided to go all in on that opportunity.

The fourth arrived when the financial crisis of 2008 hit, forcing the company to reconsider the seventeen developmental projects it was funding. But the team didn't cut back on social media efforts, or the technology rebuild they were in the midst of, or their spend on mobile efforts. Those decisions served Flowers well for the next dozen years, which were all about social media and mobility.

The fifth wave has been all about engagement. Ironically, the first real business relationships Jim ever had—as a budding entrepreneur with one shop on the Upper East Side of New York with forty clients—inspired the company's current perspective on people. Those people weren't just customers; they became friends. They stopped in for a whole bunch of reasons: for restaurant recommendations, to pass the time while they were waiting to pick up their children from school, to make themselves a mug of coffee.

Now, forty years later, Flowers has forty million customers, and it's using technology and engagement tools to get as close as possible to the same types of relationships Jim first cultivated— albeit on a much larger scale. Those relationships have become the foundation of what the team has learned about sales: you don't have to beg people to buy from you when they realize and appreciate that you are being of service to them without expectation.

That mentality has inspired the company's approach to sympathy—it's an important time of expression and thus an important vertical for a flower company. But you can't go out and advertise, "When someone you know dies, we have cheap flowers." So Jim reached out to a friend of his, John Tesh. John is an accomplished composer, musician, and broadcaster with a daily radio show that plays on hundreds of stations across the country. "John," he said, "we'd like to be on your show, but I don't want to buy any advertising."

"Huh?" John replied.

Jim explained the idea he and his team had come up with. If they wanted to go after the sympathy category, they had to help those grieving and the people close to them. That couldn't come in the form of a radio spot—it had to be something of value: knowledge. They could do that by answering the typical, yet uncomfortable, questions that come up for those who have recently suffered a loss.

Through a series of features on John's show, 1-800-Flowers became a repository for sympathy-related knowledge, pooling the experts and using John's megaphone to connect with his community on the subject.

John will tell you that it's the most engaged his audience has ever been on a topic, because it's one that's difficult to talk about. It demonstrated, too, that the Flowers team didn't have to advertise when it came to sympathy products; they only had to serve. And when a purchase was appropriate, the company automatically had that audience's consideration. Service became their go-to-market strategy.

When St. Patrick's Day rolled around—a relatively minor holiday as far as gifting goes—the team took a similar tack: using it as an excuse to engage with customers, whom they think of more as members of their community than buyers. The company held a seventeen-day countdown to the holiday that included a call for customers to share their favorite limericks, vote on their favorite Irish novelists, and more. The company cultivated fun. And when that fun brought up warm memories of people in their lives, customers acted on them.

The Cheryl's Cookies shamrock-shaped cookies sold out five days before the holiday, even though the company didn't promote a particular sale on them or encourage customers to buy anything. Meanwhile, the team was tickled to see Irish rock bands trending on various social media channels. Jim's team is riding the wave, and gearing up for the next one, which is all about AI. To do that, they have to get in front of it early, jumping in before it's too late—just as they have embraced earlier tech-driven waves.

How do they ensure they're ready for what's coming? With what they call Kultural Kudos: recognitions that celebrate the kind of culture they want at the company and beyond. At each enterprise town meeting, the head of HR reads out the company's Kultural Kudos. Anyone can nominate another for doing something they deem worth celebrating—those who take risks and lead the charge on new activities, pioneering new products that give customers more reasons to build better, deeper relationships.

To prepare for the wave of AI, Jim asked the team who was most excited about the subject. A number of people mentioned Johnson Lu. Johnson had organized a forum to bring together people from across the organization to discuss AI, chatbots, and Large Language Models (LLMs). To encourage others to think like Johnson, his name was read as part of Kultural Kudos. Though he's not in a leadership role officially, the company will continue to celebrate the way he's leading with curiosity.

Power to the Pupils

When it comes to lifelong learning, there are few better examples than Natalia Brzezinski, a moderator, journalist, and communications strategist focused on building dynamic dialogue across industries and cultures. Natalia grew up straddling cultures. The daughter of Polish and Ukrainian immigrants who had settled in Chicago, she began teaching herself English by watching *Sesame Street.*

Her multilingual, multicultural experience came in handy as she navigated numerous roles at the intersection of digitalization and diplomacy, innovation, and leadership, from the US Senate press office, to the US embassy in Sweden, the *Huffington Post*, and her role leading global business development at the Stockholm-based financial services company Klarna.

Natalia chalks up her success to a single factor: her endless quest for self-improvement. Her parents instilled in her the importance of determination, resilience, and drive—regardless of circumstance—and she continues to follow their lead today.

She is proof that the power of lifelong learning is undeniable. The process of acquiring knowledge, skills, and values throughout one's life, often beyond formal education, allows you to adapt to changes and challenges—both personally and professionally. Lifelong learning enables people to stay relevant in their fields, identify and harness new opportunities, and pursue their passions. Natalia's ongoing quest for personal growth and self-awareness has given her the chance to explore new interests, expand her knowledge base, and develop a greater understanding of herself and the world.

As a testament to her belief in always bettering herself, Natalia is brushing up on her French to better assist her global clients.

Between meetings and motherhood, you just might find her on the Duolingo and Babbel language apps. When you run into her, be sure to greet her with "Comment ça va?" Then, let her know where your quest for knowledge is taking you.

LESSONS FROM THE BEST SELF-HELP BOOKS ON MAKING YOUR RÉSUMÉ A VERB

Think Again: The Power of Knowing What You Don't Know by **Adam Grant**

Before making a name for himself in academia as the University of Pennsylvania's youngest tenured professor and becoming a global authority on organizational design, Adam Grant was an ambitious, small-town kid from West Bloomfield Township, Michigan, with disparate interests. Along with an exceptional academic record, Grant received an All-American designation in springboard diving in high school and taught himself magic tricks in his free time.

He took those interests with him when he left West Bloomfield and continued to develop them; Grant worked as a professional magician throughout his undergraduate years at Harvard University and his doctoral program at the University of Michigan, where he studied organizational psychology.

Along the way, he realized that his penchant for learning primed him for success. Further, he found that lifelong learners like him share behaviors that equip them to thrive at every phase of their existence: they find joy in the unknown, challenge their beliefs, and never attach themselves to a single identity. They constantly rethink and unlearn what they've been taught in order to free themselves from the restraint of norms and reimagine what's possible.

But it isn't without discomfort. Grant instructs that, to spark breakthroughs and progress, we must do the same: open ourselves up to the risks that come with learning, train ourselves to become uneasy with the easy, and—perhaps most importantly—be willing to be wrong. He writes, "We learn more from people who challenge our thought process than those who affirm our conclusions. Strong leaders engage their critics and make themselves stronger. Weak leaders silence their critics and make themselves weaker."

To get better and go further, Grant invites us to seek out "challenge networks" within our communities that ask us to think critically about what we believe, how we came to believe it, and what knowledge gaps might exist in our logic.

We all have blind spots in our beliefs, but "if knowledge is power, knowing what we don't know is wisdom."

Thinking, Fast and Slow by Daniel Kahneman

In *Thinking, Fast and Slow*, Nobel Prize–winning psychologist Daniel Kahneman shares with readers a truth many find hard to believe: that there are times when we can and cannot trust our own intuition. But he offers slow thinking as a simple mind hack that can help us better discern what to do.

In the book, Kahneman outlines the two systems that drive the way we think; by understanding them, we can learn to navigate challenging situations with care, thought, and exactitude for better results.

System 1 is the fast, emotional, and unconscious mind. It can:

- Find the source of a specific sound.
- Complete the phrase "war and . . . ."
- Drive a car on an empty road.

- Understand simple sentences.

System 2 is the slow, calculating, and conscious mind. It can:
- Determine the appropriateness of a particular behavior at a party.
- Keep a faster-than-normal walking rate.
- Spot the pigeon with a shiny wing at the park.
- Parallel park in a challenging parking space.

When we learn how our minds work—and how to use them most effectively—we can improve our outcomes. The fact of the matter is that in times of high stress, our intuitive thought processes (System 1) tend to override our rational thinking (System 2). This can lead to a state where logical problem-solving becomes difficult. While System 1 can be helpful when dealing with familiar problems or situations, it lacks the capacity to effectively address novel or unfamiliar challenges.

So, "mind the gap." Slow down and increase the amount of time between impulse and action. Allow System 2 rational thought to prevail.

TWO HANDS ON THE PENCIL WITH VINT CERF

Thanks to the Internet, today's world is more connected than ever. Communication is as simple as sending an email, goods can be ordered to your door at the press of a button, and online communities have brought far corners of the world closer than ever before—but it wasn't always that way. It took many years, extensive research, and brilliant leaders to make it happen.

Vint Cerf, one of the founding fathers of the modern technology that changed the way the world lives, helped connect the
first nodes of the Internet. Vint has been awarded the National
Medal of Technology, the Turing Award, and the Presidential
Medal of Freedom, among many other honors.

Vint's career has spanned over half a century, but it started
early: while he was still in high school, he worked on NASA's
Apollo program, helping to write statistical analysis software to
test rocket engines. After studying math at Stanford, he worked at
IBM as a systems engineer supporting QUIKTRAN, an interactive
computer programming language. He left IBM to attend graduate
school at UCLA, where he collaborated on the technology that
would help bring the internet to life.

Since then, he has been a professor at Stanford University,
worked for Google as a vice president and Chief Internet Evangelist,
and served on the National Science Board. Recently, Cerf has been
working with NASA's laboratories on the Interplanetary Internet,
breakthrough technology that will help us communicate from
planet to planet using radio and laser communications.

As you can see, Vint has one of the most impressive résumés
the world has ever seen. How did one man manage to accomplish
so much? He has stressed that none of it would've been possible
without "two hands on the pencil."

What does he mean by that? He didn't do any of it alone.

It's a common misconception that the world's greatest achieve-
ments are the result of one person's efforts. But almost every significant accomplishment is the culmination of the work of a team,
each contributing their unique skills, knowledge, and experience
to reach their common goal.

Cerf knows that when people work together toward a common objective, they can leverage one another's strengths and mitigate one another's weaknesses. That leads to more efficiency and a higher likelihood of success.

It's a good reminder that most learning doesn't happen in a vacuum. Looking to others does more than expose you to their experience and expertise; it bolsters your motivation and morale and imparts a sense of belonging and purpose. Take it from Vint Cerf: no major accomplishment is achieved by oneself, and the opportunity to learn alongside one another is perhaps one of life's greatest gifts. When you tap into the resources of others, what once seemed impossible suddenly appears within reach.

LODESTAR

Dogs of all ages can learn new tricks—if they put in the effort. Try the following to ensure you're always in learning mode:

- **Ask yourself, *What's next?*** One of the best ways to ensure ongoing growth is to continually ask yourself what you'll tackle next. Is it a new language, a new sport, a new technology? When you're always seeking something new, it's nearly impossible to stagnate.

- **Work with your brain, not against it.** Our brains are primed to learn and remember best under certain conditions. If we know what those conditions are, we can adapt our approach to better absorb new information. When possible, "mind the gap" between impulse and action and allow your rational problem-solving brain to guide you.

- **Invest in learning relationships.** The best teachers can be found in and outside the classroom. It's cultivating those relationships when and wherever you find them that supports lifelong learning.

- **Bring a friend.** We accomplish so much more when we build a team that can compensate for our weaknesses, bolster our strengths, and motivate us to take it to the next level.

PART 2

CHAPTER 8

HONE YOUR EQ: EXPANDING YOUR EMOTIONAL AND SOCIAL INTELLIGENCE

*There is an old-fashioned word for the body of skills
that emotional intelligence represents: character.*

—DANIEL GOLEMAN

IT WAS A WEDNESDAY IN THE MID-1980S. A PROFESSOR FROM another highly ranked university was visiting Harvard, giving a guest lecture as part of a weekly forum. He told the story of a college student he'd met. She, the college student, was interested in a PhD program at Yale, and he thought she had exceptional potential. But when she applied for admission to the school's PhD program, she was rejected.

Apparently, her test scores didn't corroborate the exceptional potential the professor had seen. He was sure his assessment hadn't been wrong—and that those test results weren't accurate indicators of the student's true potential. Instead, he realized, what truly mattered wasn't being measured at all.

Interestingly, a few months earlier, a professor had told a very similar story in that same venue. He had met a student with incredible potential who also hadn't made the cut. Both students went on to achieve remarkable things. While a few lecture attendees may have made the connection, the convergence of these fascinating anecdotes went largely unappreciated until around 1995, when a book changed so much of what we know about individual potential.

In the previous chapter, we discussed the importance of lifelong learning, which adds to your library of cognitive resources, expands your collection of lived experiences, and allows you to adapt and innovate—all while combating the cognitive decline that often comes with age. When we think of lifelong learning, we usually think of adding facts and figures to our knowledge repertoire and enhancing the way we think. But there's another type of learning that is just as—if not more—important: emotional intelligence. It mattered for those students, who had it in abundance, and it matters for you.

WHY IS HONING YOUR EQ SO IMPORTANT?

Emotional intelligence, or EQ, refers to the ability to recognize and manage your own emotions—and the emotions of others—in positive ways.

Back to that book that changed it all: Dr. Daniel Goleman, codi-
rector of the Consortium for Research on Emotional Intelligence
in Organizations at Rutgers University, is the foremost expert on
EQ. In 1995, he published a book called *Emotional Intelligence:
Why It Can Matter More Than IQ*. That book took the notion of
emotional intelligence from obscure psychological construct to
household term, teaching the masses that emotional intelligence
means a great deal, not just for PhD admissions but also in virtually every aspect of life.

The Difference-Making Quotient
We see it play out all the time: How often have you heard of people
with incredible IQs who never lived up to others' expectations?
And on the flipside, how many times have you heard of those who
achieved extraordinary successes with less-than-extraordinary
intelligence? If you've recognized this phenomenon, you're
not alone.

The year 2021 marked the hundredth anniversary of perhaps
the most influential investigations testing the power of intelligence.
In 1921, Stanford psychology professor Dr. Lewis M. Terman identified 1,521 children who scored 135 or greater on the Stanford-
Binet intelligence (IQ) test. (For reference, those who score 130 or
above are typically labeled "gifted" or even "genius.")

These children who, on average, were born in 1910, were
fondly referred to as "Terman's Termites." Terman and his research
group followed these geniuses throughout their lives. As you
might expect, Terman's geniuses achieved certain levels of success.
But there was more to the story.

Two children who were excluded from Terman's study group
because they weren't considered intelligent enough actually went

on to win Nobel Prizes. Meanwhile, none of the individuals included in the genius group did.

An even more revealing analysis of the life trajectories of Terman's geniuses was conducted years later by Dr. Melita Oden, in 1968. The hundred most successful study participants—consisting of PhDs, physicians, lawyers, and judges—were compared to the hundred least successful, a group of salesclerks, cleaners, and technicians. On average, their IQs were the same.

So what accounted for the greater successes achieved by the first group? While everyone in the study was considered "gifted"— that is, those with the greatest aptitude—it was likely their EQ that determined their success and perhaps even their happiness.

Ultimately, EQ is becoming increasingly recognized as a critical skill in today's fast-paced and interconnected world. EQ has been linked to better mental health outcomes, including lower rates of anxiety and depression. Studies have found that individuals with high emotional intelligence are better able to manage stress, cope with negative emotions, and maintain positive relationships. They can express themselves more clearly and effectively and have better listening skills, which can lead to better relationships, both personal and professional. They can also make better decisions— ones that not only align with their values and goals but also take into account the emotions and perspectives of others.

EQ affects our work lives too. For example, a recent study by the Consortium for Research on Emotional Intelligence in Organizations found that teams with high levels of emotional intelligence had higher job satisfaction, higher productivity, and lower turnover rates. And data shows that having high EQ influences your income to boot. A study by TalentSmart found that people with high emotional intelligence make an average of $29,000 more per year than those with low emotional intelligence.[29]

And the good news is that, unlike the intelligence quotient (IQ), which was previously heralded as the number-one determinant of intelligence and is mostly influenced by genetic factors, EQ is a skill that can be developed over time. When you work to improve your emotional intelligence, you'll likely experience benefits in all aspects of your life, from the personal to the professional.

Before we get into the ins and outs of it, we must note that EQ is not about manipulating others to get what you want. It's about taking in and processing all the information available to you for your benefit and that of everyone around you.

What does EQ really entail? You have to be aware of and in control of your feelings and use them effectively to communicate to, empathize with, and influence others.

You also have to read the room, regulating and expressing your emotions appropriately in different situations. When you hone that skill, you'll also find that you've improved your relationships, decision-making skills, and overall well-being. Talk about making it happen!

The Four Spheres of EQ

So, how can you train up your EQ? Like most things in life, it takes time, effort, and maintenance—including ongoing practice and commitment—but it *can* be done at any age or experience level. As Dr. Goleman explains, there are four key domains of EQ:

1. **Self-Awareness.** The ability to read and understand your own moods and emotions and to recognize their impact on others. When we become more attuned to our feelings,

we can better manage how we respond to those around us—and do so in healthier ways.

2. **Self-Management.** This is about managing your thoughts to achieve the outcomes you want. That's easier said than done, as emotions have a tendency to send our brains in wacky directions. Goleman refers to this as the "amygdala tick," the tendency of the amygdala—a small, almond-shaped structure in the brain—to react instinctively and unconsciously to emotional stimuli. The amygdala is a key player in the brain's emotional processing and helps trigger the fight-or-flight response in response to perceived threats.

   In *Emotional Intelligence*, Goleman explains that the amygdala sometimes overreacts to emotional stimuli, leading to impulsive and irrational behavior. For example, if someone insults us or threatens us, our amygdala may immediately trigger a defensive response, even if the threat is not actually serious or imminent. That's why self-management is so important. When we learn to recognize and manage our emotional responses, we can avoid getting caught up in automatic and often counterproductive reactions.

3. **Social Awareness.** This is where reading the room comes into play; it's all about accurately assessing and inter-preting others' emotions through empathy. Both visual and verbal clues, such as facial expressions or tones of voice, instruct us on how to engage with them and influence them in positive ways.

4. **Relationship Management.** Can you take your emotions, those of others, and a particular situation into account to

manage your interactions in healthy ways? If so, you're nailing relationship management—a key tenet of conflict resolution, teamwork, and collaboration. When you master this one, you can move personal and professional interactions toward the best possible outcome.

What does high EQ look like in action? We can turn to our forty-second president for a prime example.

A Presidential Prowess for EQ

Back in the 1990s, Jim bonded with Bill Flynn, who was chairman and CEO of Mutual America at the time. As a fellow Irish American, Bill welcomed Jim into the community's social circles in New York City. During one dinner with the group, Jim got to know a fellow named Ron Brown, who was then the chairman of the Democratic National Committee. At the time, Ron was helping to run Bill Clinton's campaign—and even invited Jim to travel with the president to Northern Ireland to learn more about the business community there, along with their shared roots. It was a pinch-me moment for a kid from South Queens.

What impressed Jim most—even more than Air Force One—was President Clinton's unparalleled EQ. He was an ace at reading a room and responding appropriately to achieve his desired outcomes with friends, constituents, and even skeptics. On that Ireland trip, Clinton would speak upward of three times a day, from a morning meeting with aeronautical workers on a factory floor—tough, grizzled guys who appeared as if they'd seen and heard it all—to a hoity-toity gathering of the Irish elite at a black-tie event in the evening. By the end of his visit, each audience was eating out of his hand. He knew how to charm supporters and critics alike—including Jim's wife, Marylou.

Marylou wasn't the biggest fan of Clinton's, but at one memorable White House Saint Patrick's Day party, that all changed. As Jim and Marylou made their way down the receiving line, Clinton leaned in to speak with her, hooking his arm through hers.

"Marylou," he said, "your husband and I have had such good times together! We shared so many laughs in Ireland." In a matter of seconds, he had won her over, and Jim snapped a photo of her beaming up at him, all googly-eyed.

Knowingly or not, Clinton always put Goleman's four domains to work, maintaining self-awareness, assessing others' emotions, and tapping into the situation at hand to connect and transform. That brings us to the true Golden Rule.

The True Golden Rule

In 2018, George published a book for a very different audience than the academics he typically writes for: young children.

It tells the story of a little rabbit named Rodney. Though Rodney lived in a forest full of animals, he had no friends. Rodney asked his teacher for advice. His teacher told him that all he had to do was practice the Golden Rule of Friendship, which says, "Treat others the way you want to be treated."

So, Rodney tried that out. He quickly discovered it was not as effective as he had hoped. In fact, he became more focused on himself than ever before.

Frustrated, Rodney went to visit the wise Olivia Owl. He asked her how he could make friends. But the wise Owl had a very different take on the Golden Rule. She said it was easy, "All you have to do is practice the Golden Rule of Friendship: 'Treat others the way *they* want to be treated," she explained. Rodney quickly realized that to treat others the way *they* wanted to be treated, he would have to uncover their perspectives on life. In other words, he would have to learn to see the world through their eyes, not just his own.

As Rodney learned, the law of unintended consequences is that treating others the way you want to be treated encourages you to learn more about yourself—not others. That's not a bad thing, but it doesn't do anything to help you with social interactions. Meanwhile, as George sees it, the Golden Rule of Friendship is all about perspective-taking, or attempting to see, think about, and feel the world as others do. That requires looking outside yourself and digging into what those around you want and need. Through perspective-taking, we can all learn to become more "other-oriented" and thus become happier and more successful ourselves. It can even help us find love.

Listen for Love

It turns out that tapping into EQ might also help cultivate—and accelerate—romantic relationships.

Mandy Len Catron, a writer and teacher based in Vancouver, British Columbia, went viral for her 2015 *New York Times* piece, "To Fall in Love With Anyone, Do This." Her findings sparked a global conversation about love, relationships, and the psychology of human connection—and is backed by science and hundreds of relationship success stories.

In the piece, Catron describes an experiment she replicated in her own life: a 1997 study by psychologist Dr. Arthur Aron, whose award-winning research centers on the self-expansion model of motivation and cognition in personal relationships.[30]

Aron's process involved having two strangers ask each other a series of thirty-six increasingly personal questions and then engage in four minutes of sustained eye contact. The idea was to see if this process could create the kind of intimacy and closeness that typically takes much longer to develop.

Mandy decided to test out Aron's theory with a man she'd known for years but had never gotten close to. Over the course of an evening, they asked each other the thirty-six questions, which ranged from "What would constitute a perfect day for you?" to "When did you last cry in front of another person?" They then stared into each other's eyes for four long, silent minutes.

Just as Aron predicted, the experience was intense and emotional, and Mandy found herself feeling much closer to the man. In fact, they began dating—and they're still together today!

So, why is Aron's method so effective? The questions create a sense of vulnerability and openness between the two people, which in turn leads to a feeling of closeness and intimacy.

Mandy's thesis? Falling in love is not necessarily about finding the perfect person; it's about creating the right conditions for intimacy and connection to flourish. Her work delves into aspects of vulnerability, communication, and empathy—all skills that come part and parcel with EQ—to help us understand common relationship complexities.

While the thirty-six questions may not work for everyone, taking the time to ask someone about their hopes, fears, and dreams can help foster better relationships, deeper connections, and even love. Plus, what do you have to lose?

LESSONS FROM THE BEST SELF-HELP BOOKS ON EXPANDING YOUR EMOTIONAL AND SOCIAL INTELLIGENCE

Emotional Intelligence: Why It Can Matter More Than IQ by **Daniel Goleman**

Internationally renowned psychologist and award-winning science journalist Dr. Daniel Goleman's book *Emotional Intelligence: Why It Can Matter More Than IQ* remained on the *New York Times* bestseller list for a year and a half and has been printed in forty languages.

The *Financial Times, Wall Street Journal,* and Accenture Institute for Strategic Change have listed Goleman among the most influential business thinkers today. *Harvard Business Review* called Goleman's research "a revolutionary, paradigm-shattering idea," and the book, which recently celebrated its twenty-fifth anniversary in print, was named one of the twenty-five most influential business management books by *TIME* magazine. When it comes to EQ, he's truly the best of the best.[31]

In *Emotional Intelligence,* Goleman draws on groundbreaking brain and behavioral research to explain an interesting phenomenon: in certain work tasks, people with high IQs struggle, while those with modest IQs do surprisingly well. He drilled down further to find that those who are successful often exhibit a few key EQ factors, which include self-awareness, self-discipline, and empathy. Together, those factors add up to a different kind of intelligence—EQ—a quotient that isn't fixed at birth.

The crux of his theory is that people with well-developed emotional skills are more likely to be content and effective in their lives through "the ability to identify, assess and control one's own emotions, the emotion of others, and that of groups."

On the flip side, Goleman warns that people who cannot marshal some control over their emotional lives fight inner battles that sabotage their ability for focused work and clear thought.

Simply put, those who are unable to manage distressing emotions, have empathy, and foster effective relationships typically struggle for success—no matter how smart they are.

Fortunately, it's never too late to cultivate EQ. You can start by understanding the "two minds"—the rational and the emotional—and harnessing both to rewire the way you think.

The 5 Love Languages by Gary Chapman

In 1992's *New York Times's* bestselling *The 5 Love Languages*, Dr. Gary Chapman shares a difficult truth: maintaining healthy relationships is among humanity's most complicated tasks.

But why?

Often, the problem is in the way people communicate their love to their partners. Gestures of care and affection vary from person to person, and understanding the distinct ways one prefers to receive love is key to a healthy relationship. As Chapman explains, "In reality, relationships that are successful tend to take the attitude, 'How can I help you?' and 'How can I enrich your life?'" Sounds like the Golden Rule of Friendship to us . . .

The way someone experiences love dictates their love language, which Chapman breaks down into five distinct categories:

- **Words of Affirmation.** Sharing words or phrases with your partner to make them feel good about who they are and what they do.

- **Quality Time.** Giving your partner your undivided attention.
- **Gifts.** Selecting meaningful surprises for your loved one.
- **Acts of Service.** Helping with chores or tasks to show your appreciation.
- **Physical Touch.** Hand-holding, hugs, cuddling, and other forms of physical closeness.

Chapman shares that learning to speak your partner's love language can help you understand how to make your partner feel loved, cared for, and understood—and learning your own love language can have a positive impact on how you both offer and receive love and connection.

Through Chapman's academic background in anthropology, his research posits that, while you can't control the feelings of your loved ones, you *can* influence them—and the fail-safe way to accomplish that is by meeting your partner's needs and speaking their particular love language fluently.

It's not just about romance either. Though we're not suggesting you make a habit of cuddling your colleagues, these concepts can be applied to other relationships in your life. Taking the time to understand how people communicate and what they appreciate can go a long way in building all sorts of connections.

Emotional Agility: Get Unstuck, Embrace Change, and Thrive in Work and Life by Susan David

AWARD-WINNING HARVARD MEDICAL SCHOOL PSYCHOLOGIST Dr. Susan David theorizes that the way people engage with their emotions shapes their health, well-being, happiness, relationships—everything. In the *Wall Street Journal* bestseller *Emotional Agility: Get Unstuck, Embrace Change, and Thrive in Work and Life,* Dr. David's research finds that emotional agility—the ability to navigate and adapt to one's emotions in a flexible and constructive way—serves as a road map for "loosening up, calming down, and living with more intention. It's about choosing how you'll respond to your emotional warning system."

David's four-part approach is designed to help people understand the circumstances of any given moment, respond appropriately, and then act in alignment with their values. That includes the following:

- **Showing Up.** Instead of ignoring difficult emotions, learn to face thoughts, emotions, and behaviors willingly, with curiosity and kindness.
- **Stepping Out.** Recognize that emotions are data, not directives. Step out of the struggle against emotions and into the empowering experience of processing them.
- **Walking Your "Why".** Identify a personal set of values and use them as a compass to keep moving in the right direction.
- **Moving On.** Every person should appoint themselves as the agent of their own lives and approach their daily actions, interactions, and habits mindfully so that they can bring their best selves into the world.

Her research is designed to help readers navigate the peaks and valleys of life with determination, acceptance, and minds open to possibilities. When you do, you can "cut through the noise" of everyday life and tap into your best self with intentionality.

Navigating Partnerships with Stacey Abrams and Lara Hodgson

"I want to be president of the United States someday," Stacey Abrams finally admitted. She was at a conference with Lara Hodgson, a woman with similar ambition. The facilitator had been pushing Stacey to share something she'd never shared before, calling on her constantly, even though she hadn't raised her hand. Eventually, he broke her down.

That's not something women admit in public, Lara thought to herself as soon as Stacey said it. *I have to meet this woman.* Five minutes later, they broke for lunch and, as Lara told it during a session at Women & Worth's Summit 2023, she "accosted [Stacey] at the buffet line."

Lara said, "I'm sure she was thinking, *Who is this over-caffeinated woman that's all in my space?* We ended up in the same study group working on large-scale projects for Atlanta for the next year." By the end of the program, Lara was pregnant and looking to leave her job for an opportunity with more flexibility.

She told Stacey, "You're the smartest person I've ever met...we should do something together." Stacey agreed. They just weren't sure what yet.

As Lara explained, "The lesson in that is, if you have an amazing partner—if you have two amazing people—the idea can be average. A great idea with average people has less of a chance of success than [an average idea] with great people."

She and Stacey decided to start a consulting firm together. But they weren't exactly peas in a pod. "We had wildly divergent personalities, we have different politics, we have different backgrounds," Stacey said.

What did they share—other than IQ?

"A common belief in doing good." As Stacey explained it, "We had a common interest in trying to develop something that could solve problems. Neither of us slept very much either. And so, the company came into being because we would call each other or write each other at two in the morning." As such, they called their firm "Insomnia Consulting." Their tagline became "We solve the problems that keep you up at night."

Together they worked to reconcile their differences and use them to their advantage. "Lara has never met a stranger," Stacey said, "and I have, many times. She was much more aggressive about going out to get work. I will do all of the work I can. I'm less inclined to ask you to hire me. . . . That was one of the benefits of the partnership. She had a skill set that I didn't have, and she had a willingness to leverage that skill set." With that in mind, they landed on an agreement: "We were both going to do the work, and no matter who landed the gig, we were equally responsible."

When they did a case study for NASA, Stacey did the bulk of the writing. When they worked on a real estate project—Lara's area of expertise—Lara handled most of the work. Thanks to their agreement, they didn't waste time tallying hours. They split everything 50/50, along with what they called a "promote": whoever landed the gig got an extra 15 percent. The arrangement allowed them to do what they did best as individuals, all while tending to their unique responsibilities—Lara's as a mom and Stacey's as a government official.

"If we had to keep a count of hours or if we were ticking off who did what, [we'd] start to resent one another. But by setting the parameters early and writing it down . . . we set our expectations [up front]."

They also didn't fight over titles. Stacey was COO and Lara was CEO, and, as Stacey said, "Because we both know ourselves well enough, we didn't need the titles to tell us who we were. The titles helped other people understand how to deal with us."

What was most important when it came to managing their relationship with EQ?

"We were anticipatory, we figured out what things we were going to fight about later."

Their advice to you?

"Know what things are, figure out how you will solve them, and solve them before they become a crisis. Solve them when they're just an idea."

They also got good at having tough conversations. Lara and Stacey did infrastructure consulting, working with C. B. Richard Ellis, an American commercial real estate services and investment firm, and the world's largest zinc mine, among others.

For one engagement, they were invited to Houston to meet with a team of white men who seemed surprised to see two women show up.

"We walk into the room together, our names are on the agenda, but they only talk to Lara," Stacey said. "Anytime there was a question, if I started to interject, they would turn to Lara to get her to validate what I said. I'm fairly certain one of them wanted me to get them coffee.

"It just kept happening and I just shut down because I'm an introvert. This was an area where I was confident in my capacity, but in that space it was very clear that they had no interest in my opinion. And Lara kept answering questions because Lara solves problems. We're trying to land a client and she's doing her job, which is getting us money, and in that space, the most important thing was to land the client."

But in the car after the meeting, Lara asked how Stacey thought it had gone, and Stacey was quiet. Lara realized something was up and pushed Stacey to say something.

"Lara," Stacey responded, "you realize that not a single one of those men directly addressed me."

Lara hadn't noticed. She had entered the space knowing that, in the rarefied air of boardrooms run by men, there's an issue with gender. But she had never had to confront the issue of race. They had a conversation about how to present and validate Stacey as a woman and a Black person in a space that didn't accept the utility of those identities.

Stacey appreciated that "[Lara] didn't know what the problem was, but she knew there was a problem, and she wasn't going to let it go."

"The other thing is," Lara added, "Stacey and I often say, 'Be curious first, critical second.' That's usually the opposite in the world today. We usually see something and we immediately judge; we're immediately critical. She could have looked at me and said, 'Why didn't you notice?' She could have immediately jumped to judgment about my lack of awareness of the issue. But she didn't. She was curious first ... And that [led to] this amazing conversation around how do we [prevent] that from happening again? That's a lesson for a lot of us ... Be curious first, because there's an opportunity for growth."[32]

LODESTAR

By training up on EQ, we can lead happier, more fulfilling lives, build stronger relationships, and even influence others in positive ways. Work on honing the following approaches, and you'll be primed for positive outcomes:

- **Listen up.** Practice the pause, pay close attention to what your conversation partner is saying, and reflect back their feelings to show you understand. This skill helps you develop empathy and strengthens your ability to connect with others on an emotional level.

- **Get curious.** Asking thoughtful questions shows others that you genuinely care about their unique experiences and gives you the opportunity to learn about where they've been and where they hope to go.

- **Ask for feedback.** Feedback is key to growing our EQ and our ability to connect. By regularly checking in with others on how we respond to their emotional needs, we can improve our ability to care for and understand them.

- **Keep your emotions in check.** When we can manage our emotions, we can control them. Various techniques, including deep breathing and relaxation exercises, allow us to respond to challenging situations more effectively.

- **Learn *their* language.** Understanding how others need to feel seen, heard, and understood helps us to show real gestures of care, which lead to healthy relationships in every area of our lives.

....

CHAPTER 9

BUILD COMMUNITY: ESTABLISHING MEANINGFUL RELATIONSHIPS

The first thing we ever got when we were born was a hug,
and that's what people crave for the rest of their lives.

—MICKEY DREXLER

DR. PATRICK O'SHAUGHNESSY IS THE KIND OF GUY WHO MAKES two new friends every day before noon. He's kind and friendly and interesting and—perhaps most importantly—highly interested in you. That's not because he has too much time on his hands. He's president and CEO of Catholic Health, a $3.2 billion health system in Long Island comprising six hospitals, three nursing homes, home health services, hospice, physician practices, and a whopping sixteen thousand employees.

With so much on his plate, it would be easy to let personal relationships slide, but Dr. O'Shaughnessy is deliberate about maintaining those connections. Each year, he makes a list of the people and relationships he wants to invest in so he'll be sure to cultivate them. He's intentional about that aspect of his life, and his intentionality ensures those relationships will grow and deepen even as his professional responsibilities accumulate. And on the flip side, at the end of what looks to be a very long and successful career, those connections will still be there.

That brings us to an important truth. We've spent a lot of time discussing the ways in which we can improve ourselves and our lives. But when it comes to our happiness and our survival, relationships are vital. Even ancient thinkers such as the Roman statesman Cicero—who lived way back in the first century BCE—recognized the significance of relationships on our well-being. In his writings, Cicero points out that friends have the incredible ability to amplify our joy while also lightening our sorrows. Said another way, "Friends multiply happiness and divide sadness."

In the nineteenth century, pioneering biologist Charles Darwin shed light on the importance of healthy, reciprocal relationships within successful communities. Darwin hypothesized that these relationships could be the very fabric that holds human society together. His observations highlighted the interdependence *and* interconnectedness of individuals, and that the presence of meaningful friendships plays a crucial role in shaping communities.

Fast-forward to the twentieth century, and scientific research began unraveling the profound impact of supportive relationships on our health: It became evident that human connections were linked to both mental and physical well-being. Additionally, having strong social connections acted as the most reliable predictor of human resilience.

What does that mean for you, in particular? A whole lot.

WHY ARE RELATIONSHIPS SO IMPORTANT?

Whether in the form of profound insights from ancient philosophers, evolutionary observations of pioneering scientists, or rigorously gleaned evidence from modern researchers, the message remains clear: relationships are not a mere luxury, but a fundamental human need. They improve our health, empower us to navigate challenges, and enrich our lives. For some serious longitudinal evidence, we can turn to the Grant Study, an eighty-plus-year body of research conducted by the Harvard Study of Adult Development.

Launched by Harvard physician Dr. Arlie Bock and named after its first patron, variety-store magnate W. T. Grant, the Grant Study followed 268 Harvard-educated men (the college didn't go coed until 1971) from the classes of 1939–1944 with the goal of unlocking what contributed to happiness and healthy aging.

Scientists used various data for their research, including medical records, questionnaires, and in-person check-ins, to find the keys to living longer and better—for the entirety of nearly all of the participants' lives.

From 1972 to 2004, Dr. George Vaillant, a psychiatrist who came on board as a researcher in 1966, led the study. With his background as a psychoanalyst, Vaillant dug into the significance of the men's relationships. He eventually realized that these connections played a pivotal role in determining whether they could enjoy long and fulfilling lives. Despite varying levels of wealth, geographic location, and physical health, it was relationships that had the biggest impact on well-being.

"When the study began, nobody cared about empathy or attachment," Dr. Vaillant shared. "But the key to healthy aging is relationships, relationships, relationships."

Even good genetics proved less important than healthy and sustaining relationships for participants' overall quality of life and longevity. "The surprising finding is that our relationships and how happy we are in our relationships has a powerful influence on our health," said Dr. Robert Waldinger, a psychiatrist at Massachusetts General Hospital and a professor of psychiatry at Harvard Medical School and the current director of the study. "Taking care of your body is important, but tending to your relationships is a form of self-care too. That, I think, is the revelation."

In a TED Talk titled "What Makes a Good Life? Lessons from the Longest Study on Happiness," Dr. Waldinger explained that having strong relationships benefits not only our physical health but also our mental well-being. That doesn't mean our relationships need to be perfect all the time. In fact, even elderly couples who argue frequently can still maintain healthy memories as long as they have a deep sense of trust and support during challenging times. To understand how to develop those relationships— romantic and platonic alike—we can turn back to the ancient philosophers.

The Modern Applications of Ancient Philosophy

Aristotle was an ancient Greek philosopher and polymath who lived from 384 to 322 BCE. He made major contributions to various fields of knowledge, including philosophy, logic, ethics, biology, physics, and politics—many of which have had a profound influence on Western thought and remain relevant today.

For instance, we can use Aristotle's work to gain insight into what makes relationships tick.

Study enduring friendships and you'll find yourself probing the depths of human understanding and mutual support. But not all friendships go long—or deep. In Book VIII of *Nicomachean Ethics*, Aristotle's philosophical treatise on ethics, he describes a hierarchy of three types of friendships.

The most basic are friendships of utility. These relationships are just functional—they are a means to an end, usually some extrinsic goal or profit. They're also the most fragile. As Aristotle explained, "[Friendship] whose motive is utility have no Friendship for one another really..." (Book VIII, Chapter IV).

The next level of friendships is rooted in pleasure. These relationships are based on a form of interpersonal attraction that transcends utility, but they, too, can be shallow and short-lived, as the basis for attraction (such as physical appearance, peer group status, or athletic ability) can easily change. Both friendships of utility and pleasure exist only as long as they are reinforced by external factors.

At the top of the hierarchy are friendships of goodness or virtue. This form of friendship is more about supporting others than it is about being supported. It's fueled by the mutual desire for the other person to have "goodness"—success or happiness, for instance—in their life. That makes it intrinsically reinforced and rewarding. Aristotle called these friendships "perfect." They are the most rare but also the most enduring, as they do not depend on external rewards.

Where do your friendships tend to fall on the hierarchy? Many of us find that most of the relationships in our lives fall into the first two categories. That's particularly true for men, who—thanks to a number of factors—don't tend to go deep when it comes to platonic bonding. But it doesn't have to be that way.

Beef Up Your Friendships

Ever wonder if your friendships are the real deal or superficial connections based on convenience? It's easy to confuse acquaintances with close pals—especially in the age of social media, where worth is measured in "likes" and "follows."

Men in Western society tend to struggle most of all, feeling most isolated and thus at a heightened risk for depression, substance abuse, violence, and even suicide—all consequences of a dearth of close relationships. But it wasn't always like this.

From the days of ancient Greece up until the twentieth century, male friendships were seen as an incredibly fulfilling and important part of life. Many men were all about cultivating deep connections, open sharing, and sentimental bonds with the other men in their lives. But things started to change in the late 1800s with the rise of "traditional masculinity"—think emotional aloofness, denying distress, a strong sense of independence, competitiveness, and even a preference for being a "lone wolf." Ironically, this idea of masculinity, which aimed to reinforce male dominance in society, actually ended up messing with the development of long-lasting friendships among men and eroding their role in men's lives.

Traditional masculinity has high potential for toxicity because it stifles emotions and prevents men from relying on others, resulting in those harmful feelings of isolation. Clinical psychologist Dr. Jett Stone even coined the term "malienation" to describe this process. The historic role of men in society is now facing practical and existential crises.

It's a real challenge, but recognizing these issues and working toward change can help foster meaningful friendships among men. It's time to redefine what it means to be a man and embrace emotional openness and interdependence—for the sake of ourselves and the good of society. How do we do that?

The following five conditions have been proven to support virtuous friendships:

1. **Understanding.** Finding shared interests, lived experiences, and challenges help us grasp where the other person is coming from.

2. **Self-Disclosure.** Telling others about our lives—including the hard stuff—is one of the building blocks of strong relationships. Doing it frequently ups the impact.

3. **Trustworthiness.** Demonstrating loyalty and dependability enables others to let their guard down and put their faith in us.

4. **Support.** Leaning into the sincere desire to promote the success, happiness, and well-being of friends with no expectation of reciprocity brings us closer to true friendship.

5. **Reliability.** Being there when others need us—with consistent understanding, self-disclosure, trustworthiness, and support—secures quality relationships for the long haul.

Of course, these conditions aren't just important for relationships between men; anyone can benefit from putting these tenets to work.

Simply, virtuous relationships are fueled by the mutual desire to have "goodness"—and couldn't we all use a bit more of that?

Get Communal

Author, lecturer, and behavioral engineering expert Nir Eyal discovered a way to keep his friends close despite their busy schedules and parental responsibilities. They've formed a group called the "kibbutz," an Israeli term for "a communal settlement," where members live and work together, sharing resources and responsibilities.

Here's how it works: Four couples meet every two weeks to discuss a thought-provoking question while enjoying a picnic lunch. By having a specific topic to focus on, they can bypass small talk and delve into meaningful conversations that truly matter. This also prevents gender divisions within the group and encourages everyone to engage in the same discussion.

The kibbutz lasts for about two hours, during which time the group gains new insights and strengthens their bond. It's brought Eyal out of the funks that come part and parcel with modern life and provided him with the psychological nourishment he didn't realize he was missing.

Consistency is key for the kibbutz. They meet without fail every other week, rain or shine, at the same location. Each couple brings their own food, eliminating the need for preparation or cleanup during the gathering. If one couple is unable to attend, the others continue with the conversation.

As for kids, they are welcome to attend, but they're not allowed to take over. They play independently while the grown-ups chat, and if they interrupt, they are reminded that the adults are having "an important discussion."

In fact, the adults have actually committed to this arrangement for the sake of their children. They want to demonstrate that meaningful friendships require active listening and undivided attention—even if it means setting aside distractions such as cell phones or other obligations.

Here's how to create an Eyal-style kibbutz of your own:

- **Set your dates.** Book the time on your calendars for the foreseeable future to avoid guesswork or scheduling headaches.
- **Make it meaningful.** Choose deep topics that strengthen your bonds and avoid small talk. (In Eyal's group, a different member brings a "question of the day" to each meeting.)
- **Keep adults on the mic.** Kids benefit from seeing you model healthy adult friendships. Tell them they can listen or participate—but they can't interrupt unless it's an emergency.

By reserving time on the calendar, going beyond surface-level conversations, and demonstrating the importance of friendships to your kids, you can reap the benefits of meaningful connections—even amid the busiest of life's seasons.

A Case for the Casual

But it's not only the deepest of friendships that matter; casual interactions (think weekly pleasantries with bank tellers, kind waiters, and fellow dog parents at the local park) are more than what meets the eye when it comes to our overall health and happiness.

In a recent *New York Times* article, "They May Be Just Acquaintances. They're Important to You Anyway," Paula Span, a veteran journalist and professor at Columbia Graduate School of Journalism, says there's proof in the "Nice to see you again!" pudding.

Span explores the significance of these interactions in one's life and their impact on well-being. She highlights the experiences of individuals who have developed casual relationships with acquaintances and how these interactions contribute to their happiness and sense of connection.

In one example from Span's piece, Victoria Tirondola, Lam Gong, and Pattie Marsh met at a dog park and formed a bond through their shared love for their pets. They each live alone, but meeting regularly at the park provides companionship and a sense of belonging.

Psychologists refer to these connections as "weak ties," but their impact is anything but. "Weak ties matter, not just for our moods but our health,"[33] says Dr. Gillian Sandstrom, a psychologist at the University of Sussex. Interacting with more acquaintances has been linked to greater happiness, well-being, and a sense of belonging. Even brief conversations with strangers at coffee shops or a quick exchange with a delivery driver has been found to offer benefits. Research has also shown that weak ties can be particularly important for older adults whose social networks tend to shrink over time.

When COVID-19 disrupted these everyday interactions, it emphasized the value of weak ties, the novelty and spontaneity they bring to people's lives, and the genuine friendships that can be built from them—it's part of why we're here today.

LESSONS FROM THE BEST SELF-HELP BOOKS ON ESTABLISHING MEANINGFUL RELATIONSHIPS

Men Are from Mars, Women Are from Venus: A Practical Guide for Improving Communication and Getting What You Want in Your Relationships by John Gray

"It's just, there's all this pressure—you know? Sometimes it feels like it's right up on me, and I can just feel it. Like literally feel it, in my head. And it's relentless. I don't know if it's ever going to stop. I mean, that's the thing, I don't know if it's ever going to stop," a woman tells the man sitting next to her on a couch.

As she turns her head, we see that there is an actual nail sticking out of her forehead.

"Yeah," the man says compassionately. "Well, you do have a nail in your head ... "

"It is not about the nail!" she responds.

"Are you sure, because I bet if we got that out of there ... "

"Stop trying to fix it!" she chastises.

"No, I'm not trying to fix it, I'm just pointing out that maybe the nail is causing ... "

"You always do this! You always try to fix things when what I really need is for you to listen!"

As soon as he acquiesces to her request, acknowledging, "that sounds really hard," the woman's tone shifts entirely.

"It *is* hard. Thank you!" she says, gazing at him like he really gets it for the first time.

Then they go in for a kiss and bump into the nail.

"If you ... "

"Don't!" she says.

In this popular 2013 skit, filmmaker Jason Headley shines a comical light on a common battle between the sexes, one that John Gray explored more than a decade earlier in his book *Men Are from Mars, Women Are from Venus* (1992). *Men Are from Mars, Women Are from Venus* serves as a guide to understand the differences between men and women and offers suggestions for improving communication between the sexes in both personal and professional relationships. The book has gone on to sell over fifteen million copies and is widely reported as the highest-ranked nonfiction book of the 1990s.

Gray's theory posits that men and women have fundamentally different communication styles and needs, which can lead to misunderstandings that result in emotional misfires and avoidable disasters. He suggests that men tend to be more focused on achieving goals and solving problems, while women are intent on nurturing relationships and connecting emotionally with those around them. Jim has seen this reality play out more than once: when his wife, Marylou, shares a struggle, his first instinct is to fix it. But often, all she wants is a listening ear.

So, if the sexes are so different in how they approach the complexities that foster meaningful relationships, is there a way to level the playing field?

John says, "You bet!"

Men Are from Mars, Women Are from Venus offers practical advice for bridging these differences, such as learning to communicate in a way that is more effective when connecting with those different from you. Here are the key takeaways from this seminal work, inclusive of all genders and planets:

• Love thrives when we accept our differences.

- We empower one another when we learn how to communicate effectively and motivate our partners.
- We have different intimacy needs and "score relationship points" in different ways.
- When difficult emotions arise, it's important to communicate effectively, as arguments ruin relationships.
- Knowing when to ask for support can keep your relationships thriving.

Long story short: when you make an effort to understand and appreciate the unique qualities and needs of your partner, everyone wins.

Games People Play: The Psychology of Human Relationships by Eric Berne

Psychiatrist Eric Berne's *Games People Play* is considered the first popular psychology book of its kind. Published in 1964, it explores the intricacies of social interactions and sheds light on the psychological games that we engage in to fulfill our emotional needs—and even manipulate others.

The book delves into a wide range of psychological games that people play in their relationships. Berne explains the motivations behind these games and how they contribute to the perpetuation of unhealthy relationship patterns. But we can break free of these destructive games with awareness and conscious decision-making. By recognizing and challenging the games you play, you can achieve more genuine connections and improve overall well-being. It starts with developing a clearer understanding of your own emotional needs and engaging in authentic, open communication to foster healthier relationships.

GETTING NEIGHBORLY WITH SHANNON BREAM

You've probably heard the proverb "Good fences make good neighbors," and while there may be some truth there, there's a great deal of good in store for those willing to welcome connection— whether it's at the local supermarket or just over the property line.

Journalist and author Shannon Bream understands the powerful role her local community has had in her life and the transformative realization that came to her during the COVID-19 pandemic.

While most regard the early days of lockdown as a dark time, and often rightly so, she discovered a bright spot among the growing global fear.

Like many, Shannon found herself on Zoom calls with family and friends as the pandemic began—occasionally with a glass of wine in hand—to check in and foster a sense of togetherness in isolation. But to her surprise, it was her neighbors—and their capacity for care in the face of uncertainty—who inspired her most and restored her faith in the world.

Shannon witnessed her community truly looking out for one another—sharing groceries, caring for the elderly among them, and stepping into what she refers to as "caretaking and investing mode." Those she once perceived as strangers were now "checking on each other's lives and connecting."

Even Shannon's husband, Sheldon, jumped in on the community building happening on their block. "When it snows, he's the first one out there shoveling everybody's driveways. He loves doing that for our neighbors and strangers, too, and spreading this good cheer through the neighborhood."

Shannon notes that, while folks might have differing viewpoints on social and political issues, it's a human duty to care about one another. We can't just "pick and choose who we're going to be kind to," she said.

Rather, to understand those in our communities and show true empathy, we must embrace many different kinds of people in our lives. And there are many ways that we can love one another and build relationships. For so many of us, COVID-19 demonstrated that we're called to do just that.

LODESTAR

Here's what you'll need to make relationships of all stages and types meaningful:

- **Remain open.** Whether you're chatting up a new acquaintance or sharing a meal with an old friend, stay engaged and inquisitive—and share a bit of your life too. You never know where a conversation may lead or when a connection might spark.

- **Stay supportive, without thinking of reciprocity.** This is the cornerstone of what Aristotle called "the perfect friendship."

- **Look locally.** Remain open to the community around you, and don't be afraid to get neighborly—be it in the cul-de-sac, coffee shop, or at the fence line. Looking out for our community members boosts morale and makes us feel safe.

CHAPTER 10

....

ASK FOR HELP: GETTING THE SUPPORT YOU NEED, WHEN YOU NEED IT

Asking for help isn't a sign of weakness, it's a sign of strength. It shows you have the courage to admit when you don't know something, and to learn something new.

—BARACK OBAMA

IT WAS 1967. A TWELVE-YEAR-OLD BOY IN MOUNTAIN VIEW, California, was working on a project—an electronic frequency counter—in his garage. Things were going swimmingly, until he got stuck. He realized that to complete the device, he needed more parts, but they were hard to get ahold of (there was no such thing as "buy with one click" back then).

There was only one person he could think of who would have the parts—and they weren't exactly close. The boy opened the Palo Alto phone book and ran his finger down the page. He doubted he'd find the name he was looking for, but there it was, nestled between Heston and Heyward. Right there, in black and white, was the home phone number of Bill Hewlett, cofounder of Hewlett-Packard.

The boy picked up the receiver and dialed the number, his heart racing. Would Hewlett be annoyed that some kid was bugging him at home to give him spare parts for a stupid pet project?

He wasn't. In fact, Hewlett was so amused by the young boy's request that he not only gave him the parts, he offered him an internship on the HP assembly line.

Not long after, that boy and his friend began assembling personal computers in their garage. They dubbed their partnership the Apple Computer Company. For the rest of his life, Steve Jobs would tell the story of his phone call to Bill Hewlett and underline the importance of asking for help.

"I've actually always found something to be very true, which is most people don't get those experiences because they never ask," Jobs said in a 1994 interview.[34] "I've never found anybody who didn't want to help me when I've asked them for help."

The first nine chapters of this book are about ways you can help yourself and improve your life.

This one is not.

While we'd love to say the advice in this book will solve all your problems, that would be foolish. Yes, you do have an obligation to take care of yourself the best that you can, and yes, the techniques in this book will help you do that. But the reality is that you can't tackle all your issues alone. Sometimes, you need to ask for help.

The problem? Making the request taps into our deepest-seated fears about our self-worth. We worry that it makes us appear weak. It deals a blow to our egos and forces us to question our abilities. If we need someone else to assist us, are we really as competent as we thought we were?

Plus, it's easy to feel like when we ask someone for help, we're putting them out or bothering them. We feel as if we're being given charity, that we're somehow taking without properly reciprocating. That's one of the reasons many people are willing to pay a therapist to listen to their problems but are hesitant to talk to their friends and family about them. When money is involved, it feels like a more even exchange (in fairness, a therapist may indeed have better insight than Uncle Ned, but that's a subject for another day).

The truth is, most people want to help. There's inherent value in doing the giving too.

WHY IS ASKING FOR HELP SO IMPORTANT?

The smarter and more successful people become, the more independent they tend to get. They begin to feel as if they're above help, that if they just put their head down, drop their nose to the grindstone, grab those bootstraps, and pull, they can do it. And that's where they end up falling short. No matter how hard we try, we just can't fix it all.

An associate dean of a well-known medical school once told George that smart people can do anything. Taking that to its logical extension would demonstrate that if we're smart enough, we should be able to take care of ourselves when we're sick or broken. That's just not the case. As the old maxim from Sir William Osler goes, "The doctor who treats himself has a fool for a patient." One should not attempt to perform surgery on themselves—or cut their own hair, for that matter. Some things are best left to the pros.

By refusing others' help, we severely limit our ability to heal and grow. We miss opportunities to connect with others—and, by the same token, we rob them of the chance to feel good about themselves.

Get a Second—or Third—Opinion

If you're willing to get a second opinion about fixing your car or your dishwasher, why wouldn't you when it comes to the most important thing in your life—yourself!?

Trying to solve problems yourself fails to take into account the vast amounts of information and expertise out in the world. You often lack the outside perspective necessary to solve a problem yourself—the "forest for the trees" concept. Getting additional opinions can help shine a light on your blind spots and make you more self-aware.

Do-it-yourselfers run into this problem all the time. Sure, they may save money and walk away from a project with a sense of pride, but the true cost often outweighs the cash and warm fuzzy feelings. Which is safer and more effective in the long run—learning to wire your house from a YouTube tutorial or hiring a licensed electrician to do the job for you?

Another reason many decide to go it alone is because subconsciously, they feel that asking for help means they must cede control to someone else. George sees this worry often during his work with the military and first responders—both fields attract very control-oriented people.

It may feel as though you're giving your control to someone else when you employ their help, but it's important to remember that no matter what the situation, you still have agency.

Remember too: just because you're asking for someone else's opinion or assistance doesn't mean you have to take it! In 99 percent of situations, you can choose to participate or not. George once needed to undergo a medical procedure. On the day of the surgery, he put on his gown and was wheeled into the cold operating room, and right before the surgeon began, George held up his hand.

He said he had some questions about the procedure and the aftereffects, and the surgeon gave him an answer he didn't like. He got off the operating table, changed out of his gown, and left.

If anything, asking for help gives you more control. The more questions you ask, the more information you receive, which results in a more informed choice.

When it comes to making important decisions, George lives by the maxim he calls Everly's Law of Three. Always get three opinions. You can employ this in your life and gain—not lose—control.

Boost Their Ego
Worried you'll be a burden while working up the nerve to ask? The simple truth is that people like helping people.

A Stanford University psychology study found that those needing help consistently underestimated others' willingness, underestimated how positively helpers would react, and overestimated how inconvenienced helpers would feel.[35]

This is because helping others boosts our self-worth. In his book *Magic Words: What to Say to Get Your Way*, Dr. Jonah Berger writes that by asking someone for assistance, you're implying you value that person's judgment, experience, and knowledge. In essence, you're stroking the person's ego and making it personal, which makes them more willing to help.

What else makes people more willing to help? Admitting you need help!

Demonstrating your vulnerability from the outset of an interaction opens your audience up to giving you what you need. Master negotiator Chris Voss calls this concept the Accusation Audit, which he developed during his years as a professional hostage negotiator for the FBI. The Accusation Audit entails preempting the potential negative reaction you think others will have about your request.[36] The classic example of this is prefacing an ask by saying, "I hate to do this to you, but ..."

By disarming the potential objections ahead of time, you'll not only feel better about the ask because you've addressed the elephant in the room (or in your mind), but you'll also set up a more empathetic conversation.

Don't Ask for Help—Recruit It

Getting the help you need means you have to jump those hurdles that your ego places in your path. One way to do that is to reframe it within your own mind.

In its common form, *asking* for help is a submissive activity. We mentally associate it with helplessness, like crying out for a lifeguard when we're drowning. In those situations, we're forced to admit we cannot swim on our own and need someone to save us.

It's the same dependence you felt as a child. You needed adults to help you tie your shoes or reach for an item on a high shelf. The power imbalance you felt made you feel subservient to others.

That's fine when you're a toddler, but society dictates that as you get older, you're supposed to become more independent and rely less on others. You're taught that persistence and effort are the right ways to get by, and anything else makes you less successful, less competent, less...

Instead of spiraling into a vortex of negative self-talk, don't think about it as *asking* for help—think about it as *recruiting* help. "Recruit" is an active word. It conveys agency and control. The process is very much the same, but the simple act of reframing can completely change your attitude toward it.

Practice, Practice, Practice

Like any other skill, asking for help requires repetition. As licensed clinical professional counselor Myron Nelson points out in *Psychology Today*, asking for—and accepting—help takes practice.[37] The more you do it, the less discomfort you'll feel as you begin to understand that your fears about what could go wrong (embarrassment, shame, ridicule—just to name a few) are unfounded.

Nelson recommends measuring your improvement by how the person you're asking responds and whether or not you receive the help you need.

Another way to practice is by increasing the number of questions you ask people. We often frame "help" as making a request that requires people to go out of their way for us, but it could be as simple as providing their opinion or expertise.

Above all, the most successful people are the ones who understand and accept that they don't have all the answers and who seek out information from those who can help.

Do Your Homework First

As we've noted, the benefits of asking for help far outweigh the disadvantages. We always hear the advice "it can't hurt to ask," but are there times when asking for help is *not* appropriate?

Timing certainly matters. What might seem like an emergency to you might not be urgent to the person you're asking for help. For example, as a college professor for fifty years George has often had students ask questions in the middle of a lecture that are unrelated to the topic under discussion at the moment. You can't get upset when you ask for help in the wrong situation and the person you're asking doesn't drop everything for you. Use your social awareness to decide if it's a good time to go in for the ask.

Make sure to exhaust other options too. Have you sincerely tried to solve the problem yourself first, whether that means doing a quick Google search or hoofing it to the library? Attempting to get all the info you can—and demonstrating that you've done your homework—goes a long way toward reaching your end goal and informing your recruit that you care about their time.

In the early days of 1-800-Flowers, Jim had an office manager ask him to help select an office copy machine. "I don't know anything about copiers," she confessed.

Jim, who didn't know much about copiers himself, affirmed that the manager was a very smart person, and told her that if she called various copy machine companies and asked questions, she would likely learn all that she needed to know in order to make an informed decision.

Put Yourself out There

Essentially, we're talking about putting yourself out there at the right time—and with the right background information—and trusting others to be kind about it. The reality is, when it comes to being vulnerable, our fears rarely come to fruition. Instead, we're presented with the opportunity to harness the best parts of life.

Recently, a friend of Jim's—a high-profile PR executive—had a choice to make. His nine-year-old granddaughter wanted him to try out for a show called *Generation Gap*, an ABC game show where family members from different generations work together to answer questions from different time periods. "It'll be fun, Grandpa!" she said.

But many of his colleagues warned against it. They said that the show was silly and the potential for embarrassment was high. Did he really want to risk his reputation for some stupid game show?

The man weighed his options. Yes, the chance of embarrassment was enormous, but could he pass up this opportunity to do something special with his granddaughter?

The pair arrived at the TV studio in the Bronx at 6:30 on a Sunday morning. He later told Jim that the day was long and exhausting, involving multiple wardrobe changes and, yes, lots of silly games. But they both had a wonderful time. At the end of the taping, he leaned down to his granddaughter, hugged her, and told her he loved her.

"You always say that, Grandpa," the girl said.

"Because I always mean it," he replied. "And I want to say it to you every time we're together, because someday, it will be the last time I say something to you."

His granddaughter looked up at him and smiled. "The last thing Grandma said to me was 'I love you,'" she said.

He'd put himself out there, risked embarrassment, and asked a lot of questions when it came to what elementary-age kids are into these days. All that openness paid off in spades.

LESSONS FROM THE BEST SELF-HELP
BOOKS ON EXPANDING YOUR EMOTIONAL
AND SOCIAL INTELLIGENCE

Give and Take: Why Helping Others Drives Our Success by
Adam Grant

As you will recall from chapter 7, Adam Grant is an organizational psychologist and professor at the Wharton School of the University of Pennsylvania. Grant is known for his research and writings on work motivation, leadership, and the psychology of success. Grant's work focuses on understanding how people can find fulfillment and success in their personal and professional lives.

In his 2013 *New York Times* bestseller, *Give and Take: Why Helping Others Drives Our Success*, Grant explores the concept of reciprocity and its impact on individual and collective success. He argues that people can be broadly classified into three categories: givers, matchers, and takers.

Here's the breakdown:

- Givers have a natural inclination to help others—without expecting anything in return.
- Matchers seek a fair and equal exchange of favors. These are Law of Reciprocity fiends.
- Takers are primarily focused on maximizing their personal gains, often at the expense of others.

Grant delves into extensive research and real-life examples to demonstrate that, contrary to popular belief, it is the givers who often achieve the most success in various domains of life—including work, business, and personal relationships. By consistently helping others and creating a culture of generosity, givers build strong networks, enhance their reputations, and gain access to valuable resources and opportunities.

The book provides practical strategies for navigating the challenges that givers face, like avoiding burnout and preventing exploitation by takers. Grant emphasizes the importance of setting boundaries, giving strategically, and identifying the right recipients to maximize the positive impact of one's generosity.

Grant also presents evidence-backed insights on how organizations can cultivate a culture of giving, fostering collaboration, innovation, and productivity among employees. He outlines methods for identifying and nurturing givers within the workplace and discusses the implications of creating environments that discourage takers and encourage giving behaviors.

But the biggest takeaway is that givers aren't the doormats of the world; they actually reap several key benefits that contribute to their success:

1. They build better reputations by fostering authentic relationships—and wider networks too.
2. Givers seek potential in *everyone*, which can often lead to surprising outcomes like job opportunities, friendships, and support systems when the going gets tough—unlike matchers and takers, who generally undervalue those who can't offer an immediate social reward.
3. Safe spaces are created by givers in collaborative relationships and environments, which leads to greater trust and a sense of belonging and community.

By illustrating the success stories of people and organizations that prioritize generosity, Grant encourages readers to reevaluate their approach to interpersonal relationships and work dynamics, offering a compelling case for how helping others can ultimately lead to personal (and collective) fulfillment.

Never Split the Difference: Negotiating as If Your Life Depended on It by Chris Voss

Never Split the Difference offers a unique perspective on the art of persuasion and emotional intelligence based on the author's experience as an FBI hostage negotiator.

Drawing from real-life scenarios and high-stakes situations, Voss shares practical strategies and psychological insights to help readers become more effective negotiators in both professional and personal contexts—to help them get into (and out of) just about anything.

The book challenges traditional negotiation approaches and introduces the concept of tactical empathy, which involves understanding and influencing the emotions and motivations of others.

Voss emphasizes the importance of active listening, building rapport, and demonstrating empathy to establish trust and create a cooperative atmosphere. "Persuasion is not about how bright or smooth or forceful you are," he says. "It's about the other party convincing themselves that the solution you want is their own idea. So don't beat them with logic or brute force. Ask them questions that open paths to your goals. It's not about you."

Throughout the book, Voss presents several techniques that will make others more willing to help you. Here are a few:

1. **Tactical Empathy.** Empathy, when deployed effectively, is likely to form a bond that can sway a tough debate in your favor.

2. **Mirroring in Conversation.** Mirroring builds rapport, fosters trust, and creates a sense of connection by subtly imitating the other person's behavior and language patterns.
3. **Labels.** Using labels, which are questions starting with phrases such as "it sounds like/seems like/looks like," not only make your prospect feel heard and important but also help overcome communication barriers and extend the conversation.

Voss offers a compelling blend of tactical advice and psychological strategies that challenge conventional negotiation wisdom, no matter the severity of the circumstance. By emphasizing the power of empathy, active listening, and strategic communication, readers are equipped with the tools and mindset necessary to get the help they need.

ANSWERING QUESTIONS WITH MICKEY DREXLER

It wasn't unusual to hear a disembodied voice echoing through the halls of J. Crew's corporate offices, requesting anyone and everyone's attention. It belonged to the company's CEO, Mickey Drexler, who installed the public address system shortly after taking the helm.[38]

Day in, day out, the so-called Merchant Prince used the loudspeaker to address his employees. Sometimes he announced meetings or quarterly earnings; sometimes he mused on pop culture or a dream he had the night before. Most of the time, though, he asked questions. That was his shtick, a way to deal with the *shpilkes*—the Yiddish word for "ants in your pants"—that kept him on the move and after the next big thing in fashion.

He was well-known for entering J. Crew retail locations unannounced and peppering both employees and customers with questions about the merchandise. "Which pattern do you like more?" he'd ask, or, "What do you think about the price of these pants? Is it too high?"

Drexler would do the same with J. Crew's vendors. *New Yorker* writer Nick Paumgarten once followed Drexler and his design team to a potential supplier's facility in Maine. The company made totes, duffels, and dopp kits out of old sails, and Drexler was choosing items to sell in the J. Crew catalog.

As the writer put it, Drexler turned to the bags' designers and released a deluge of questions. "Where in the world do you sell your bags? Is there an iconic or famous Sea Bag? In five years, do you repeat? Is this your logo? Do we have time to do this today? Can we just work? Should we just grab the things we like?"[39] It was just his way.

Those kinds of questions have helped him navigate career ups and downs, such as landing big retail wins—including founding Old Navy and Madewell—and moving on from major losses—such as leaving his post as CEO of The Gap and J. Crew after downward trends in performance.

In 2019, he joined his son Alex Drexler and former J. Crew and Madewell creative director Somsack Sikhounmuong to grow Alex Mill, a company Alex had founded in 2012 to create the perfect shirt. While he is no longer at the helm of J. Crew, Drexler's penchant for questions continues. He continues to prefer input over output, knowing that each question he asks of his suppliers, employees, and customers helps him make better decisions. "I go to whoever knows more than me about a subject," he said.[40]

LODESTAR

Doing it yourself feels heroic and may be a boost to your ego—but no one can do it all. The smartest, most successful people are the ones who harness the power of asking others for help. Here's how to do it well:

- **Follow Everly's Law of Three.** Whenever you need to make a big decision, get three opinions and make a more informed choice. Remember: just because you ask for advice doesn't mean you're obligated to act on it!

- **Reframe your ask.** Flip your mindset on asking for help from passive to active. You're not getting someone's permission or asking them to save you—you're recruiting their assistance because you are in charge.

- **Stroke their ego.** Asking someone for help makes them feel good. People like helping people, and by asking, you are implying that you value their experience, judgment, and opinions. If you're afraid of them responding in a negative way, preempt those negative responses by using Chris Voss's Accusation Audit strategy.

- **Put yourself out there.** You'll never know unless you try. All the fears you have about a potential situation are nothing but inventions of your own mind. Put yourself out there, ask questions, and you'll be surprised at the beautiful moments life will reward you with.

- **Perhaps most importantly, remember that asking for assistance helps others, not just yourself.** When you have an important decision to make, it's never just about you. Every important decision in your life affects and reflects on those who care about you and those who depend on you. Whether it's a business decision or a personal decision—especially personal health-care decisions—do it for them!

CONCLUSION

The only journey is the journey within.

—Rainer Maria Rilke

We're all on a quest to better ourselves. We can't help it—it's been wired into our brains since we lived in caves. It's why the self-help industry has been a part of our culture since the dawn of the written word and continues to bring in billions each year.

We love to think that because we're in the modern era, we are somehow smarter or more advanced than our ancestors—and sure, the world has changed since Aristotle mused about life's challenges and opportunities some two thousand years ago. But when we examine the themes and concepts that history's most prominent figures struggled with, we find they're shockingly similar to our own battles with self-discovery and self-improvement.

It's the reason the books we've shared with you continue to be perennial bestsellers. Their themes are universal and continue to stand the test of time—regardless of how much research was involved. Some of the principles are admittedly based on archaic norms or are justified by spiritual or psychological concepts that modern medicine has since debunked. But at their core, they work. They capture or align with some part of the human experience. And that makes them powerful.

As the old saying goes, those not familiar with the past are doomed to repeat it. And by learning from the journeys of those who came before us, we can take what we need to propel ourselves forward. The philosophers, celebrities, and thought leaders we've shared here have blazed a trail for us, removing roadblocks we'd otherwise have to learn to hurdle ourselves.

Though we delved into ten distinct areas of self-improvement, there are several overarching themes embedded in every single one of them. We've taken you through a lot of concepts, but if you leave with nothing else, hold on to these.

Mindset Is Everything

As Joan Didion once wrote in her book *The White Album*, "We tell ourselves stories in order to live." For us to make sense of the world, we must construct a narrative in our own heads, scratching out a mental screenplay of our lives with ourself as the hero. Just like that screenwriter, we are in charge of our own story. We often feel as though what happens to us is out of our control, like we're just sacks of meat bumping through our daily lives. While it's true that we can't control every aspect of our environment, we can absolutely control how we think, feel, and react. That's a concept the Stoic philosopher

Epictetus was talking about around 100 CE when he said, "It's not what happens to you, but how you react to it that matters." By shifting our mindset, we can find power in pain, turn losses into lessons, and create victories from the ashes of defeat.

Practice Makes Progress

The importance of practice is drilled into our brains from a very early age. We understand that the more we do something, the stronger we get. Lift a heavy weight, and the muscles grow so the load feels lighter. Slack off and those muscles shrink. But we often forget that the brain operates in the exact same way. By exposing ourselves to stress and uncomfortable situations in a controlled, repetitive manner, our muscles grow. This isn't just a metaphor—it's the concept of neuroplasticity that we've mentioned several times over the course of this book. With practice, the brain literally rewires its neural pathways to fast-track certain thought patterns that can contribute to or hinder your success. Just like a tough day at the gym or training for a marathon, there will be setbacks—soreness, injuries, inclement weather. Some days, wrestling with these strategies will feel so hard you'll want to stay in bed. When that happens, give yourself some grace. Arnold Schwarzenegger was once frail, Barack Obama was once an unknown junior senator from Chicago, and the Beatles once played concerts for barflies in dank Hamburg clubs. Everyone starts somewhere, and your journey to becoming a self-help superstar won't happen overnight. Get back on the road and keep going. It's practice that will ultimately get you to the destination.

RELATIONSHIPS MATTER

Yes, this book is all about improving yourself, but contrary to the moniker, self-help takes more than just you. Growth doesn't happen in a vacuum. Countless studies have shown that relationships with others lay the best path to a life well-lived and are the best single predictor of human resilience. Investing in relationships has countless benefits. We all have mental and emotional blind spots, and a trusted friend or a professional can shine a light on areas of your life that you could never discover by yourself. Sharing your journey and struggles helps you see them in a new way, and it also helps others because they can learn from you.

The friendship that we the authors, Jim and George, share is a perfect example of the power of relationships. We're just a couple of guys who connected over the Internet, and a mutual admiration for each other's lives has blossomed into a fulfilling friendship. It also resulted in the book you now hold in your hands. It is an example of remaining open to the opportunities the future can hold that were never planned or even anticipated.

A final word before we send you on your way: while we hope this book has taught you some important lessons about how to thrive and flourish—and maybe even given you some warm, fuzzy feelings—simply reading these words on the page isn't enough. Self-help is a wonderful genre of books that has no doubt changed millions of lives. Ironically, one of the reasons that bookstores dedicate entire sections to self-help is because those seeking improvement in their lives can become addicted to reading them. They close one book inspired to change, but once that feeling of inspiration dissipates, they read another and another, hoping to find that same spark.

It's not necessarily that the next book will be better than the last, but that the reader expects the book's wisdom to transform their lives through osmosis. It doesn't work that way. No amount of reading can transform your life. To see any real improvement, you must take the principles contained within and *act* on them. You must make it happen.

You wouldn't expect a hammer and saw to build your house for you—you need to take them in your hands and build it yourself. The concepts in this book are exactly the same. Consider this book a giant toolbox full of the instruments needed to construct your ideal life. You must pick them up, swing them, use them. It might mean you'll get covered in sawdust or bash your thumb every now and again, but if you keep hammering, keep cutting, and occasionally ask a buddy to hold the flashlight for you, you can build the life you want.

Of course, when the going gets too tough, it's also OK to call an expert carpenter in for help (if you read the last chapter, you already know that). We'd love to continue to guide you along the way.

The time is now. You have the tools. Pick them up and get to work. We'll be here, cheering you on.

ACKNOWLEDGMENTS

I WOULD LIKE TO THANK MY MENTORS WHO IN THEIR OWN WAYS contributed to this project: Daniel Girdano, PhD (University of Maryland); Theodore Millon, PhD, DSc (University of Miami and Harvard Medical School); Douglas Strouse, PhD; Jeffrey T. Mitchell, PhD; David McClelland, PhD (Harvard University); Stanley Platman, MD, MA (The Johns Hopkins Medical System), Jon Links, PhD (The Johns Hopkins Bloomberg School of Public Health); Michael Kaminsky, MD, MBA (The Johns Hopkins School of Medicine); Bertram Brown, MD, MPH (former director, The National Institute of Mental Health); and lastly to my friend Dennis McCormack, PhD, plank-holder US Navy SEAL Team 1, you will be missed.

—GSE

NOTES

1 "Self-Help Books Statistics," Wordsrated, December 16, 2022, https://wordsrated. com/self-help-books-statistics.

2 John Milton, *Paradise Lost* (London: Penguin Classics, 2003).

3 Eleanor H. Porter, *Pollyanna* (New York: Bantam Books, 2006).

4 Jack Zenger and Joseph Folkman, "The Ideal Praise-to-Criticism Ratio," *Harvard Business Review*, March 15, 2013, https://hbr.org/2013/03/the-ideal-praise-to-criticism.

5 Zameena Mejia, "How Warren Buffett's Optimism Has Helped Him Succeed, According to Psychology," CNBC Make It, September 4, 2017, https://www. cnbc.com/2017/09/04/how-warren-buffetts-optimism-has-helped-him-succeed-according-to-psychology.html.

6 https://www.cnbc.com/2017/09/04/how-warren-buffetts-optimism-has-helped-him-succeed-according-to-psychology.html

7 Helen Keller, "Optimism: An Essay," in *The World I Live In*, ed. Roger Shattuck (New York: New York Review Books Classics, 2003).

8 Hiroko Tabuchi, "How CVS Quit Smoking and Grew into a Health Care Giant," *New York Times*, July 11, 2015, https://www.nytimes.com/2015/07/12/business/how-cvs-quit-smoking-and-grew-into-a-health-care-giant.html.

9 Jayne O'Donnell, "A Year Later, CVS Says Stopping Tobacco Sales Made a Big Difference," *USA Today*, September 3, 2015, https://www.usatoday.com/story/news/2015/09/02/cvs-stopping-tobacco-sales/71606590.

10 Nate Skid, "How Danny Meyer Turned Shake Shack into a $500 Million Burger Empire," CNBC Make It, March 23, 2021. https://www.cnbc.com/video/2021/03/23/how-danny-meyer-turned-shake-shack-into-a-600-million-burger-empire.html.

11 Diana Drake, "Lessons from Shake Shack Founder Danny Meyer, with a Side of Fries," Wharton Global Youth Program, February 27, 2023, https://globalyouth. wharton.upenn.edu/articles/entrepreneurs-leaders/lessons-from-shake-shack-founder-danny-meyer-with-a-side-of-fries.

12 "The Right People Make the Right Decisions, The Age of Ideas," https://theageo-

fideas.com/someday-sermon-right-people-make-right-decisions.

13 Barbara Booth, "Shake Shack's Danny Meyer Changed the Restaurant Industry by Breaking All the Rules. Here's How," CNBC, February 15, 2019, https://www.cnbc.com/2019/02/15/shake-shacks-meyer-changed-restaurant-industry-by-breaking-the-rules.html.

14 Jay King, "Twenty Years Later, Rick Pitino's 'Not Walking through That Door' Rant Lives On," The Athletic, February 28, 2020, https://theathletic.com/1639350/2020/02/28/rick-pitino-celtics-oral-history/.

15 Richard G. Tedeschi and Lawrence Calhoun, "Posttraumatic Growth: A New Perspective on Psychotraumatology," Boston University Office of Research 21(4), April 1, 2004, https://www.bu.edu/wheelock/files/2018/05/Article-Tedeschi-and-Lawrence-Calhoun-Posttraumatic-Growth-2014.pdf.

16 "The Story of Michael Milken: The Junk Bond King," Gentleman's Journal, February 15, 2024, https://www.thegentlemansjournal.com/article/story-michael-milken-junk-bond-king.

17 Milken Center for Advancing the American Dream, https://www.mcaad.org.

18 The Giving Pledge, https://givingpledge.org.

19 Jeffrey A. Sonnenfeld and Andrew J. Ward, "Firing Back: How Great Leaders Rebound after Career Disasters," Harvard Business Review, January 2007, https://hbr.org/2007/01/firing-back-how-great-leaders-rebound-after-career-disasters.

20 Sonnenfeld and Ward, "Firing Back."

21 Sonnenfeld and Ward, "Firing Back."

22 Tracy Jan, "How a Yale Professor's Viral List Pressured Companies to Pull Out of Russia," Washington Post, March 11, 2022, https://www.washingtonpost.com/business/2022/03/11/sonnenfeld-russia-ukraine-corporations.

23 Jan, "How a Yale Professor's Viral List."

24 Jan, "How a Yale Professor's Viral List."

25 Ron Shaich, "Establish a 'No Jerks' Standard So We Can Start Tackling America's Real Challenges," LinkedIn, April 6, 2016, https://a3h-content.s3.us-east-2.amazonaws.com/old_articles/2d0c500107.pdf.

26 Shaich, "Establish a 'No Jerks' Standard."

27 Ron Shaich, "Hate Has No Home at Panera," August 16, 2017, https://a3h-content.s3.us-east-2.amazonaws.com/old_articles/48075c6036.pdf.

28 "Meet Ron," https://www.ronshaich.com/meet-ron.

29 "Emotional Intelligence: What It Is and Why You Need It," World Economic Forum, February 13, 2017, https://www.weforum.org/agenda/2017/02/why-you-need-emotional-intelligence.

30 Mandy Len Catron, "To Fall in Love with Anyone, Do This," New York Times, January 9, 2015, https://www.nytimes.com/2015/01/11/style/modern-love-to-fall-in-love-with-anyone-do-this.html.

31 "About," Daniel Goleman, https://www.danielgoleman.info/biography.

32 "Level Up: Scaling Your Business and Career in Today's Economy," Worth Media, YouTube, https://www.youtube.com/watch?v=g7pwE_ekB94.

33 https://www.nytimes.com/2023/04/22/health/seniors-acquaintances-happiness.html

34 "Seve Jobs on Failure," Silicon Valley Historical Association, YouTube, https://www.

youtube.com/watch?v=zkTf0LmDqKI&t=6s.

35 Xuan Zhao and Nicholas Epley, "Surprisingly Happy to Have Helped: Underesti-mating Prosociality Creates a Misplaced Barrier to Asking for Help," *Psychological Science* 33 (10), https://journals.sagepub.com/doi/10.1177/09567976221097615.

36 Chris Voss, "Tactical Empathy," MasterClass, https://www.masterclass.com/classes/chris-voss-teaches-the-art-of-negotiation/chapters/tactical-empathy.

37 Myron Nelson, "Why You Can't Ask for Help," *Psychology Today*, June 30,2022, https://www.psychologytoday.com/us/blog/how-be-burden/202206/why-you-can-t-ask-help#:~:text=Asking%20for%20help%20is%20a%20skill.,less%20and%20less%20over%20time.

38 Nick Paumgarten, "The Merchant," *The New Yorker*, September 13, 2010, https://www.newyorker.com/magazine/2010/09/20/the-merchant.

39 Paumgarten, "The Merchant."

40 "Fmr. J. Crew CEO Mickey Drexler on Alex Mill Outlook, Retail Competition, and Earnings," CNBC Closing Bell, April 18, 2023, https://www.cnbc.com/video/2023/04/18/fmr-j-crew-ceo-mickey-drexler-on-alex-mill-outlook-retail-com-petition-and-earnings.html.